Journey of a Celtic Soul

Allen Hartley

Journey of a Celtic Soul

Copyright © 2014-2016 Allen Hartley
All rights reserved.

Cover Design, Artwork, and Illustrations
Copyright © 2012-2016 Vanessa Thiele and Allen Hartley
Used Under Express Permission of Vanessa Thiele

First Printing May 25, 2016
Second Printing August 2, 2016

ISBN-10: 1503309770
ISBN-13: 978-1503309777

"A soul's outcome in the afterlife is based on knowledge."

"How well the deceased person had established truth in his lifetime against the powers of evil is the question that lies ahead in the afterlife."

"Did the deceased embrace life enough to be able to live again in death?"

"Did the deceased develop a strong enough character to continue his personality?"

Thoth

"There is wisdom in a raven's head."
Gaelic Proverb

"Three candles that illuminate every darkness: Truth, Nature, and Knowledge."
The Triads of Ireland

"Knowledge is the food of the soul."
Plato

CONTENTS

1	The Journey Begins	1
2	Seasons, Cycles, and Celebrations	7
3	Otherworld	31
4	The Soul	55
5	Ancestry	65
6	Nature	103
7	Magick	145
8	Warriors and Weapons	167
9	Runes	195
	About The Author	277

Other Books In Printed and Kindle Format By The Author

Secrets of the Soul

Mists of Dawn

Boundaries of Time

Nature's Palette: Waterscapes

ACKNOWLEDGMENTS

Once again, I thank my bonded companion, Vanessa for her insight, energy, and effort she put forth to help me complete this work. We have known and been a part of each other's lives over countless iterations.

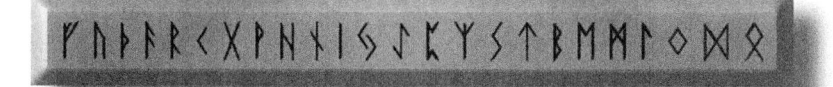

Chapter 1
The Journey Begins

I have traveled through endless dimensional universes. Mine is an old soul that has experienced many lives over countless iterations. Each traversal affords the opportunity to increase knowledge, skills, and powers. The iterations experienced on this earth are special. So special that we have a "veil of forgetfulness" placed over our souls at birth. We don't remember our past lives or accomplishments. Those that listen closely and "burn" the veil off can access their past. This veil is like the shell of an egg that the hatchling breaks. The young birds that break out of the shells without assistance are stronger.

It is absurd to think we can learn all there is to learn and master the skills we need to progress to higher levels in the brief period of ONE lifetime. Why do certain souls, places, activities, stories, smells, etc. seem so familiar? Why do certain people seem to accelerate in given areas? Why do others want to master something, but struggle? If they persist, many times they will prevail. We're able to accelerate in certain areas because we developed the skills and knowledge in prior lifetimes. As we develop additional skills and knowledge in this life, we will accelerate in those areas in the next life.

Life doesn't end with death, except in certain circumstances. Many wrongfully see death as a final state or worse, a time of reward and eternal bliss. Death is a transitional doorway. For most, it is a one way door, for others, it is not. Once certain barriers have been crossed, a return isn't usually allowed through this portal. If one is to return, it will be through the established process of birth, preserving the sacred cycles.

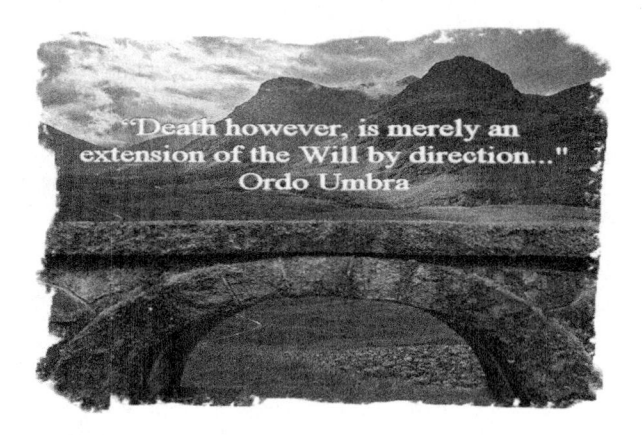

> "Death however, is merely an extension of the Will by direction..."
> Ordo Umbra

"Ni thuigfidh tú an bás go dtiocfaidh sé ag do dhorás féin"

"You will never understand death until it comes to your own door."

"Ní féidir dul i bhfolach ar an mbás"

"There is no place to hide from death."

Anam Cara: A Book of Celtic Wisdom

There are those that can move between the worlds. Our ancient ancestors referred to this as a journey to the Otherworld and Underworld. It was a place to gain knowledge, power, and enlightenment. Only a few dare to venture into these realms. Many sacred places in our world afford portals to the Otherworld and Underworld. If one is receptive enough, these portals can be discovered. If one is strong enough, he can create them.

Certain animals serve as guides and liaisons between the physical world and the Otherworld/Underworld. The blackbird, known by the Gaelic Name as Druid Dhubh (Druid-doo) or "black druid" is one of the guides to the Otherworld/Underworld.

The blackbird sings at twilight and later. Twilight and predawn are considered the time of transition from one reality to the next. The veil between the worlds is the thinnest, allowing entry into the Otherworld/Underworld. It is a time of mental and spiritual awakening, a time to journey without our physical bodies to seek enlightenment and gifts our ancestors/others that inhabit the Otherworld/Underworld are willing to bestow upon us.

We are always on a journey from darkness into light. At first, we are children of the darkness. Your body and your face were formed first in the kind darkness of your mother's womb. Your birth was a first journey from darkness into light. All your life, your mind lives within the darkness of your body. Every thought that you have is a flint moment, a spark of light from your inner darkness. The miracle of thought is its presence in the night side of your soul; the brilliance of thought is born in darkness. Each day is a journey. We come out of the night into the day. All creativity awakens at this primal threshold where light and darkness test and bless each other. You only discover balance in your life when you learn to trust the flow of this ancient rhythm. The year also is a journey with the same rhythm. The Celtic people had a deep sense of the circular nature of our journey. We come out of the darkness of winter into the possibility and effervescence of springtime.

Anam Cara: A Book of Celtic Wisdom

This book is a collection of my impressions, knowledge, memories, and feelings spanning many lifetimes. Many of these strongly identify with the Northern Celtic and Nordic traditions. I have many more journeys to make in this life and future lives.

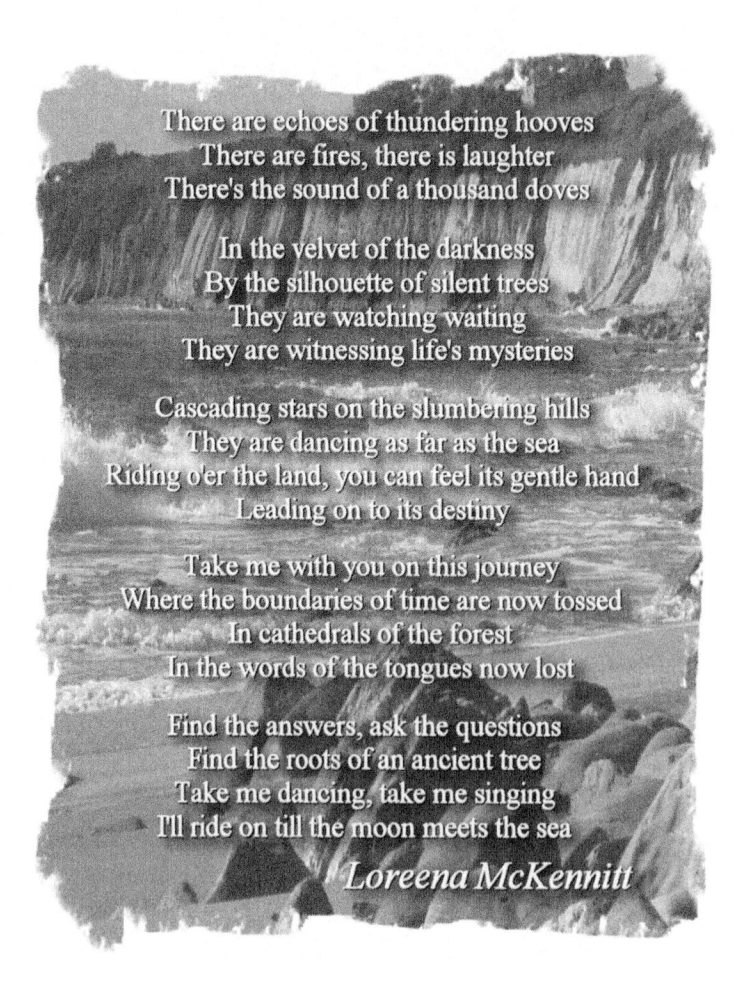

There are echoes of thundering hooves
There are fires, there is laughter
There's the sound of a thousand doves

In the velvet of the darkness
By the silhouette of silent trees
They are watching waiting
They are witnessing life's mysteries

Cascading stars on the slumbering hills
They are dancing as far as the sea
Riding o'er the land, you can feel its gentle hand
Leading on to its destiny

Take me with you on this journey
Where the boundaries of time are now tossed
In cathedrals of the forest
In the words of the tongues now lost

Find the answers, ask the questions
Find the roots of an ancient tree
Take me dancing, take me singing
I'll ride on till the moon meets the sea

Loreena McKennitt

I Choose

To live by choice, not chance,
To be motivated, not manipulated,
To be useful, not used,
To make changes, not excuses,
To excel, not compete

Self esteem, not self pity
To listen to my inner voice,
   not the random opinions of others

To do the things you won't,
   so I can continue to do
   the things you can't

"A soul's outcome in the afterlife is based on knowledge."

"Knowledge gives the power to act in truth and causes life, while ignorance blinds the sight and causes death"

"Did the deceased develop a strong enough character to continue his personality?"

Thoth

Allen Hartley

*If life doesn't bring us together
Then death won't separate us*

Chapter 2
Seasons, Cycles, and Celebrations

Standing between two wildfires built at the portals to the Otherworld, I feel winter's grip reaching for the land. My soul feels the shift of the universe as the solstice approaches. The dimensional portals open to receive the energies I release upon my enemy as the nine oil soaked cloths, etched with Runes, are ignited. The four elements are united with my soul. The winter drizzle has paused for the ceremony as the cold northern air flows down through the land. Hungry flames flare up as they feed upon the oil soaked fabric. One by one, the Runes are released into the Otherworld from this tiny northern grove. Over many lifetimes I have released energies against my enemies with the sacred Runes. As the flames finish their meal, the tiny grove is bathed in the restrained light and warmth of the two wildfires. Eventually, the wildfires fade and the portals close as snowflakes float softly to the ground.

Seasonal Compass

The Runes, like the seasons, have many faucets. My soul has always started with the sacred season of winter. There are four cycles/seasons that have been appointed to our iteration. For various reasons more were added over the centuries, but in the natural order, there are only four.

The seasonal compass marks the four cycles/seasons and their associated Runes. The center of the compass is emblazed with the Rune, ᛋ, Jara/Ár. It is the Rune of cycles and changes; life cycles, lunar cycles, seasonal cycles, the vortex of cycling energies.

Each of the compass points are marked with the Bind Runes associated with the season. Bind Runes are created by combining two or more individual Runes to create a new Rune. The combined energies can enhance, compliment, amplify, or cancel certain or all aspects of the combined Runes. Many times combining two Runes will create more than just two Runes/energies to deal with. The more Runes combined, the more complicated the energies. In some cases, undesired side effects may be encountered.

The year is a circle. There is the winter season, which gives away to the spring; then summer grows out of spring until, finally, the year completes itself in the autumn. The circle of time is never broken. This rhythm is even mirrored in the day; it, too, is a circle. First, the new dawn comes out of the darkness, strengthening toward noon, falling away toward evening until night returns again. Because we live in time, the life of each person is also a circle. We come out of the unknown. We appear on the earth, live here, feed off the earth, and eventually return back into the unknown again.

Anam Cara: A Book of Celtic Wisdom

Winter

The start of the year begins with the winter solstice and is the top most point of the seasonal compass. The two Runes, | Isa/Íss and ↑ Nauthiz/Nauð are combined into the Bind Rune, ↑.

Isa/Íss is the Rune of binding. In nature, ice creeps up on the land, quietly freezing and immobilizing everything in its path. The unaware fall victim to it. Íss freezes action and is the rune of cold, barren stillness, and death.

Nauthiz/Nauð is the Rune of endurance and will, the mental strength to last. It represents the dark night of the soul. It gives defiance and the strength to carry on when all hope seems lost. It is the Rune of survival and fearlessness in the face of death. It is also the Rune of suffering and hardship, trial and testing, and developing the will and self-sufficiency.

The Birch tree is associated with the winter season and represents renewal, rebirth, and inception. The Birch is the first tree to come into leaf after the winter season. This slender, determined tree represents the seed potential of all growth and is hardier than the mighty Oak. It signifies cleanliness and purity.

In the Druid tradition, this is the time of death and rebirth. The sun appears to be abandoning us completely on this longest night. The year is reborn and a new cycle begins. It will reach its peak at the time of the summer solstice and once again return to this season of death and birth.

There comes a time when summer asks, "What have you been doing all winter?"
Unknown

One of the traditional winter solstice celebrations is the Yule log. A log that is from one's own land, or a gift, is burned in the fireplace. It is ignited from a piece of last year's Yule log. This symbolizes the light that is passed from one year to another. The Yule log is slowly burned for 12 days and then extinguished. The ashes are stored to mix with the seeds during the spring planting. A portion of the log is preserved to light the Yule log during the next solstice.

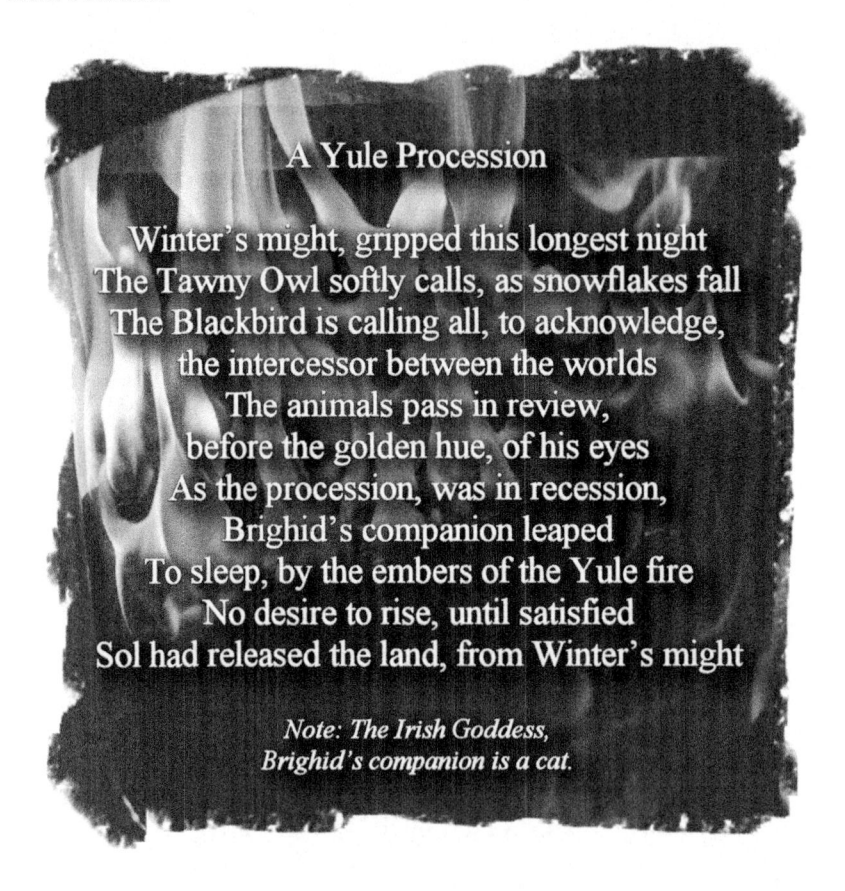

A Yule Procession

Winter's might, gripped this longest night
The Tawny Owl softly calls, as snowflakes fall
The Blackbird is calling all, to acknowledge,
the intercessor between the worlds
The animals pass in review,
before the golden hue, of his eyes
As the procession, was in recession,
Brighid's companion leaped
To sleep, by the embers of the Yule fire
No desire to rise, until satisfied
Sol had released the land, from Winter's might

*Note: The Irish Goddess,
Brighid's companion is a cat.*

The word Yule has several suggested origins; from the Old English word, geõla, the Old Norse word jõl, a pagan festival celebrated at the winter solstice, or the Anglo-Saxon word for the festival of the winter solstice, Iul, meaning wheel. In old almanacs, Yule was represented by the symbol of a wheel, conveying the idea of the year turning like a wheel.

The spokes of the wheel, were the old festivals of the year, the solstices and equinoxes. The winter solstice, the rebirth of the Sun, is an important turning point, as it marks the shortest day when the hours of daylight are at their least. It's also the start of the increase in the hours of daylight, until the summer solstice when darkness becomes ascendant once more.

Snow

White are the far-off plains, and white
The fading forests grow;
The wind dies out along the height,
And denser still the snow,
A gathering weight on roof and tree,
Falls down scarce audibly

The road before me smooths and fills
Apace, and all about
The fences dwindle, and the hills
Are blotted slowly out;
The naked trees loom spectrally
Into the dim white sky.

The meadows and far-sheeted streams
Lie still without a sound;
Like some soft minister of dreams
The snow-fall hoods me round;
In wood and water, earth and air,
A silence everywhere.

Save when at lonely intervals
Some farmer's sleigh, urged on,
With rustling runners and sharp bells,
Swings by me and is gone;
Or from the empty waste I hear
A sound remote and clear;

Allen Hartley

The barking of a dog, or call
To cattle, sharply pealed,
Borne echoing from some wayside stall
Or barnyard far a-field;
Then all is silent, and the snow
Falls, settling soft and slow.

The evening deepens, and the gray
Folds closer earth and sky;
The world seems shrouded far away;
Its noises sleep, and I,
As secret as yon buried stream,
Plod dumbly on, and dream.

Archibald Lampman

Spring

    I stand in the snow on a northern plain and feel the shifting of the season towards spring. The cosmos responds to the subtle adjustment of our world. I feel the energies of the lengthening days and the stirrings of the quiescent life buried in winter's sleep. Soon, the stillness will be disrupted as all respond to the call of spring.

    The vernal equinox is represented on the seasonal compass by the Runes, X Gebo/Gjöf and ᛒ Björk/Bjarkan to form the Bind Rune ᛤ.

    Gebo/Gjöf is the Rune of gifts and giving. As Sol diminishes winter's grip, we receive the gift of another season. The slumbering inhabitants emerge from their wintry retreats to embrace the warmth of the sun.

    Björk/Bjarkan is the Rune of fertility, birth, and nurturing. It is a powerful feminine Rune.

Birds of Spring

The birds of spring call,
for winter's thaw
Long has been their flight,
to greet winter's blight
The trees awaken, after being shaken,
by the warm breezes
From its slumber, the sun lumbers,
into the sky
The sun's rays, causes the plants to raise,
their arms in praise
As winter makes a hasty retreat,
all turn to greet, the birds of spring

As the sun grows warmer, its energies encourage the rebirth of another season. The daffodils and crocuses spring up, followed by a procession of lilies, mosses, and mushrooms. The birch and willows push their shoots upward, reaching to embrace Sol. Newborns spill forth upon the land, greeted by the songs of the birds.

When one flower blooms it is spring everywhere.

Anam Cara: A Book of Celtic Wisdom

One of the mysteries of Druidry is the Druid's egg. Life-giving, it is the egg protected by the hare, which is the symbol of spring. This is still celebrated with the giving of Easter eggs by the Easter bunny.

The celebration of Easter coincides with the Vernal Equinox. At this time, day and night are of equal length. The season is associated with goddess of fertility, Astaroth/Ashtar. She was known as Eastre to the Anglo-Saxons and is associated with rabbits/hares and eggs. Other names for this celebration include: Eohs, Eostre, Ester, Estrus, Oestrus, Oistros, and Ostara.

The hare was regarded as the symbol of fertility by our ancestors and associated with the moon. The date for Easter is determined by the moon, which is associated with the feminine aspect.

The egg represents the symbol of birth, life, and rebirth. "Omne vivum ex ovo" – "All life comes from an egg."

The goddess, Eastre represents the sunrise, spring time, fertility, and the renewal of life. The Anglo-Saxons made offerings of colored eggs to her at the Vernal Equinox.

> When in the springtime of the year
> When the trees are crowned with leaves
> When the ash and oak, and the birch and yew
> Are dressed in ribbons fair
>
> When owls call the breathless moon
> In the blue veil of the night
> The shadows of the trees appear
> Amidst the lantern light
>
> We've been rambling all the night
> And some time of this day
> Now returning back again
> We bring a garland gay
>
> Who will go down to those shady groves
> And summon the shadows there
> And tie a ribbon on those sheltering arms
> In the springtime of the year
>
> The songs of birds seem to fill the wood
> That when the fiddler plays
> All their voices can be heard
> Long past their woodland days
>
> And so they linked their hands and danced
> Round in circles and in rows
> And so the journey of the night descends
> When all the shades are gone...
>
> Loreena McKennit

Spring Tree

The tree's friend, the wind,
freed him from winter's mantle
In reply, he winked his sleepy eye
Stretching forth his branches,
he reached for the sky
Waving goodbye, to his friend

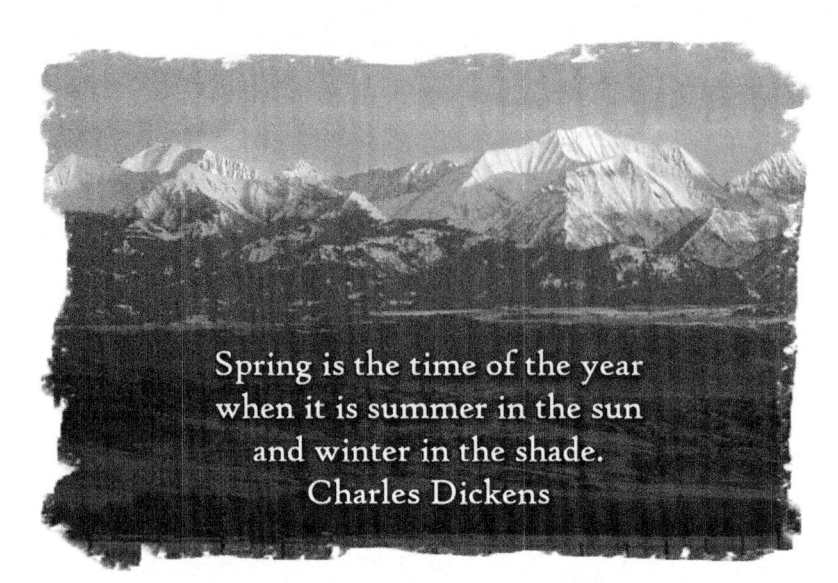

Spring is the time of the year
when it is summer in the sun
and winter in the shade.
Charles Dickens

Summer

Long before I feel the climax of the summer solstice, I feel the shift of the cosmos as our world moves towards autumn. The summer solstice is the mid-life point of the seasonal progression and is a very important time for us, as it was for our ancestors. Spring brought the promise of rebirth; summer brings the promise of vibrant life and abundance.

Light is the mother of life. The sun brings light or color. It causes grasses, crops, leaves, and flowers to grow. The sun brings forth the erotic charge of the curved earth; it awakens her wild sensuousness.

Anam Cara: A Book of Celtic Wisdom

In the coolness of the early morning, the staccato calls of the birds announce the beginning of another day. The deer snorts his approval as he moves deeper into the forest. As the day heats up, angry clouds threaten to disgorge their contents upon the land. Daytime moves towards the evening as Sol descends from his throne. The melodies of the crickets and frogs greet the twilight as the coolness creeps upon the land, diminishing Sol's touch. The centurions of darkness swoop on silent wings to their lofty outposts. Howls and yelps punctuate the nocturnal sonata until the soft hues of the predawn light slowly consumes the stars and heralds the approach of a new day.

> Green was the silence,
> wet was the light,
> the month of June
> trembled like a butterfly....
> Pablo Neruda

The summer solstice on the seasonal compass is represented by the Bind Rune ᛕ, which is created from the two Runes, ᚠ Fehu/Fé and ᛋ Sowilo/Sól.

ᚠ Fehu/Fé represents cattle or gold – transitory wealth. Our ancestor's wealth was proportional to the size of their herds. The herds could be purchased or redeemed with gold. Winter had passed, spring brought new offspring and vegetation to graze upon, and summer allowed all a time to flourish. The potential harvest in the fields determined IF our ancestors would have sufficient stores for the coming winter and surpluses to sell. The circumstances of the seasons to follow were foreshadowed by the conditions at the summer solstice.

> Summer has now thrown open her emerald doors. Every part of the landscape is profuse in leaves and flowers, and "green-robed senators of mighty woods" are clothed in their most elegant array.
> Unknown

ᛋ Sowilo/Sól is the Rune of the sun. It is also the Rune of movement and action representing a season opposite to the winter solstice – a balance of the seasons. Like ᛃ, Jara/Ár, ᛋ, Sowilo/Sól is associated with rotational motion. It was viewed by our ancestors as a spinning solar wheel.

> What good is the warmth of summer, without the cold of winter to give it sweetness.
> John Steinbeck

The summer solstice is the longest day of the year - time of maximum light, when the countryside is colorful and fragrant.

> I almost wish we were butterflies
> and liv'd but three summer days
> - three such days with you
> I could fill with more delight
> than fifty common years
> could ever contain.
> John Keats

This high day was traditionally celebrated in the forest with picnics, games, and a large bonfire. It's also the time of waning strength for Sol as the season advances back towards the winter solstice. At the solstices, the sun is revered at the point of its maximum power at the noon of the year when the days are the longest and at the point of its apparent death in midwinter.

Solstice is from Latin and is made up from two words given roughly as: sol = sun and stice = stopped. Celtic Druids do not believe that the sun stops so they use the old Irish word, Tairisem, which means standing still. In summer, this sun standing happens in the month of June around the 20th, 21st or 22nd when they honor Éatain Eachraidhe (the rider of horses), the white mare goddess. This is the highest point of the solar year when the sun reaches it maximum height in the Sky. The sun is at its highest at noon and shadows are at their shortest.

In antiquity, midsummer fires were lit in high places all over the countryside. In some areas of Scotland, Midsummer fires were still being lit well into the 18th century. This was especially true in rural areas, where the weight of reformation thinking had not been thoroughly assimilated. It was a time when the domestic beasts of the land were blessed with fire, generally by walking them around the fire in a sun-wise direction. It was also customary for people to jump high through the fires, folklore suggesting that the height reached by the most athletic jumper, would be the height of that years harvest.

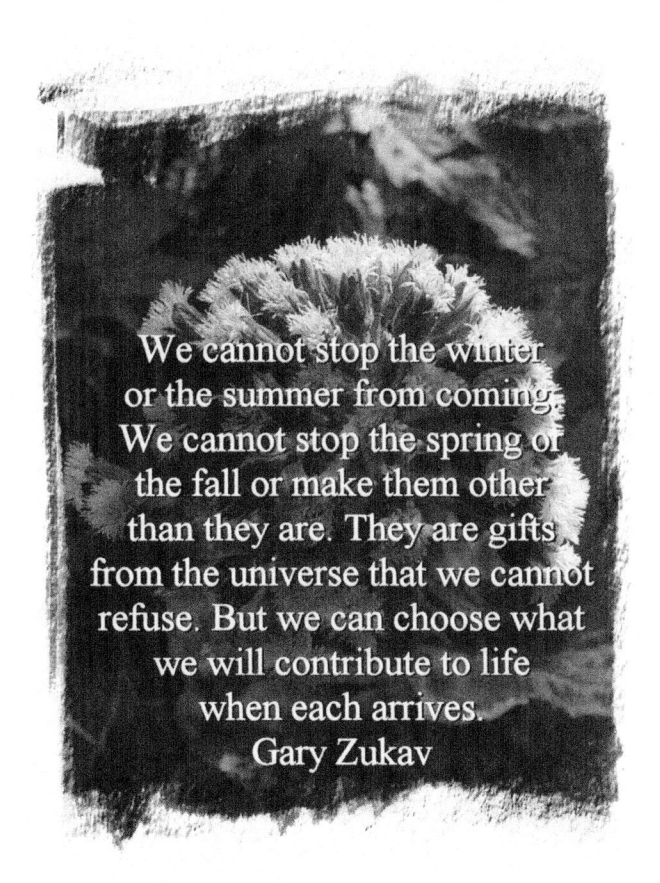

> We cannot stop the winter or the summer from coming. We cannot stop the spring or the fall or make them other than they are. They are gifts from the universe that we cannot refuse. But we can choose what we will contribute to life when each arrives.
> Gary Zukav

Allen Hartley

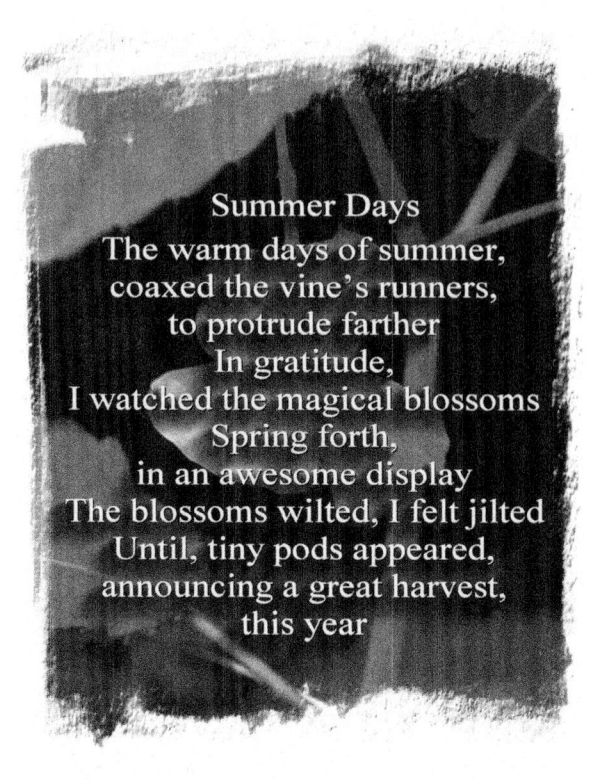

Summer Days
The warm days of summer,
coaxed the vine's runners,
to protrude farther
In gratitude,
I watched the magical blossoms
Spring forth,
in an awesome display
The blossoms wilted, I felt jilted
Until, tiny pods appeared,
announcing a great harvest,
this year

Fall

Just before the summer solstice, I feel our world moving towards the autumnal equinox. This movement accelerates after the solstice as we transition to the golden time of the year. Even though the winter solstice is months away, I can feel its presence along with the shifting of Sol's energies and our world that will complete the cycle. The seasons are symbolic of our iterational cycles – birth, childhood, adulthood, and death. As we progress through our lives, the cycles repeat like the seasons.

The Bind Rune ◊ represents the autumanal equinox and is composed of the Runes, ◊ Ingwaz/Ing and ↑ Eihwaz/Eoh.

◊ Ingwaz/Ing represents the seed or sack for seeds. Active power, the summer's growth is converted to potential power, the seed that will sprout in the spring. It's the time of year that all prepare for the long winter by harvesting and storing provisions.

Am fear nach dèan cur sa Mhàrt,
cha bhuain e san Fhoghar.
He who will not sow in March
will not reap in autumn.

↓ Eihwaz/Eoh is the rune of death and power over the dead. As life begins to wane, the promise of life is realized in the seeds produced in autumn. To live again, we must pass through the portal of death, the winter solstice. Order must be maintained and the cycles honored. Failure to do so leads to chaos and undesirable results in the natural order. The dimensional universe will rebalance the order, abruptly if needed.

The natural order is simple. All but humans flow with the natural order. Many are not aware of the natural order or ignore it. A continued ignorance of the natural order will bring a harsh correction from the dimensional universe.

At the autumnal equinox the sun wanes, as the dark half of the year draws near. As with the Vernal Equinox, day and night are of equal length. This balance in nature presents a powerful time for magick.

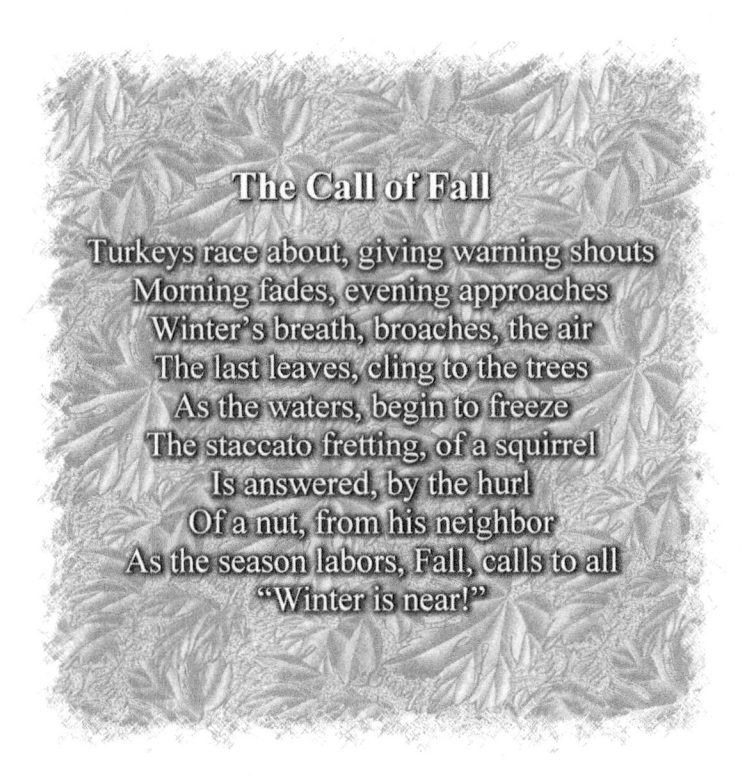

The Call of Fall

Turkeys race about, giving warning shouts
Morning fades, evening approaches
Winter's breath, broaches, the air
The last leaves, cling to the trees
As the waters, begin to freeze
The staccato fretting, of a squirrel
Is answered, by the hurl
Of a nut, from his neighbor
As the season labors, Fall, calls to all
"Winter is near!"

To the ancients, this was a sacred time. The Irish saw this time of year as the Waning of the Goddess. From the summer to the winter solstice, they would hold festivals for the God who was seen as a dark, threatening being. In Ireland, the autumn equinox was celebrated long before the arrival of the Celtic tribes. The best known of the ancient Irish equinox temples is Knowth, which is near Newgrange (Brú Na Boinne). Knowth has a 100-foot long passage that accepts the Sun on the morning of the spring and Autumn Equinox. A second and older stone Cairn equinox temple is found at Longhcrew and is given the name Cairn T. Both Knowth and Cairn T allow a sunbeam on the morning of the spring and autumn equinox to enter a passageway to light upon the sacred geometry on a back stone inside the temple. This is precise timing from a period of over six thousands years ago and it still works today.

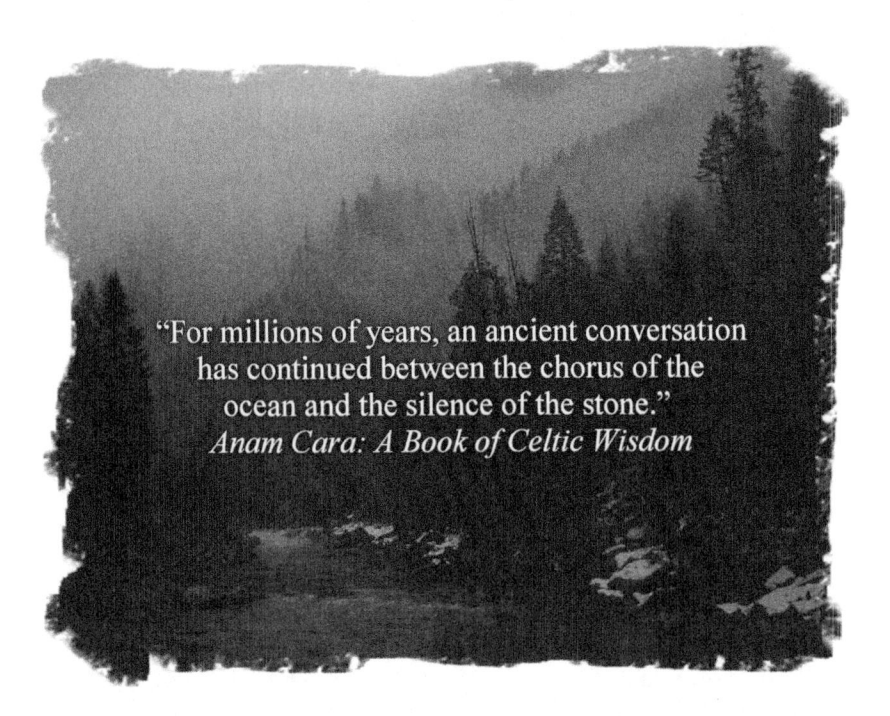

"For millions of years, an ancient conversation has continued between the chorus of the ocean and the silence of the stone."
Anam Cara: A Book of Celtic Wisdom

Fall

The gusty bluster, acts as a duster,
to the leaves, from the trees
The animals, hasten their pace,
against winter's race
The Sun's sad face,
casts long shadows
Soon it will be noon,
then night will fall
While all, wrap themselves tight,
against winter's might

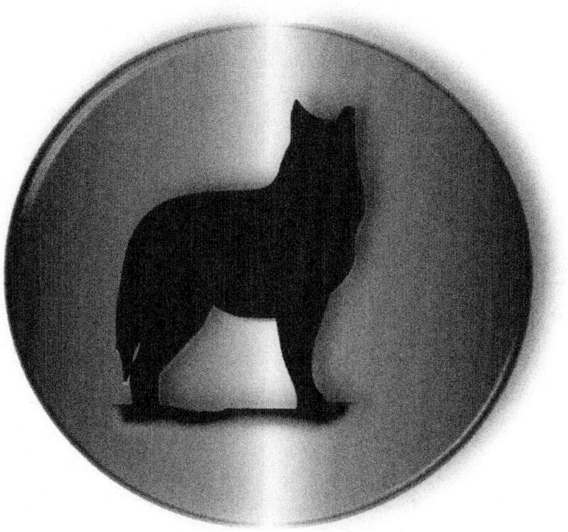

Allen Hartley

Chapter 3
Otherworld

The cool evening breeze brushes against my skin. Dark clouds obscure the full moon, casting murky shadows on the land. I feel my soul pulled inward as the energies transform my body into the sleek form of a black wulf. The cool evening breeze rushes through my fur as I race off into the night. I jump through a portal into the Otherworld and speed down a long tunnel. My focus is an enemy from multiple iterations. Tonight, I will rid myself of this enemy, never allowing her to return.

I track her energies to a large cliff with a shallow cave. She senses my presence, but can't see me. Through progressive stages of neglect over the iterations, her ability has been diminished. The blindness of her soul has been accelerated in this iteration. Although she can no longer see my vibrational energies, her intuition screams something is near. Slowing I approach, watching her every move. I sense her fear. Groping the wall behind her as she moves to the back corner of the cave, panic washes over her. Lunging, I shred her soul, never to return.

The Otherworld is a special dimension that we, like our ancestors, can release magickal powers and energies. Additionally, we can obtain knowledge, power, gifts, and commune with our ancestors that have not returned for their next cycle in an iteration. Not all are prepared or are willing to travel to the Otherworld. The journey can be difficult without a guide, but not impossible. Those with a strong soul can traverse the Otherworld. Those with a strong guide can traverse it until their soul has strengthened.

The journey is a personal, individual experience. Many have had their souls closed through religious indoctrination, peer pressure and influence, and worst of all, the pollution from our current society and media. An Otherworld journey is NOT a passive activity like watching a movie or reading a book. Like any journey, it requires planning and preparation.

There are many sacred guides that can aide the Otherworld traveler. The blackbird, known by the Gaelic Name as Druid Dhubh (Druid-doo) or "black druid" is one of the guides to the Otherworld.

The blackbird sings at twilight and later. Twilight and predawn are considered the time of transition from one reality to the next. The veil between the worlds is the thinnest, allowing entry into the Otherworld. It is a time of mental and spiritual awakening, a time to journey without our physical bodies to seek enlightenment and other gifts our ancestors, as well as others that inhabit the Otherworld are willing to bestow upon us.

Travel to the Otherworld is facilitated by the use of a Bind Rune and a strong soul. This Bind Rune was created utilizing six Runes. Each of the Runes has a specific purpose. Combined into a Bind Rune, their energies are united, enhanced, and amplified to ensure safe and successful travels between the worlds.

The Rune Kenaz/Kaun ᚲ represents the light of the soul and intellect. The traveler to the Otherworld uses it to illuminate the path and to guide them on the journey. On the journey, it provides awareness and insight. This Rune is also representative of the unity between our iteration and the Otherworld – the living and the dead. Ourselves, our ancestors, and those yet to return to another iteration. It is also a very powerful Rune for penetration. In this case, penetration of the veils between our iteration and the Otherworld.

Ansuz/Óss ᚠ represents the spoken and unspoken words of magick used in our journeys between and through the Otherworld. Ansuz/Óss is used to enhance psychic and magickal abilities. It allows communion with those we meet in the Otherworld. Not all that is communicated is done verbally. Nothing is more powerful than the spoken words of magick, except those with the focus and ability to direct magickal energies silently with their soul.

Raidho/Reið ᚱ is the actual journey between this iteration and the Otherworld. It is the Rune of travel, journeys, and physical endurance. It also represents seeking the unknown, a journey/step into the unknown. Through this Rune, one can understand the rhythm and flow of the dimensional universe. This Rune is used to ensure a successful journey through the Otherworld and to ensure a successful return to our iteration. Without this Rune the traveler will be at the mercy of a multitude hardships.

Thurisaz/Þurs ᚦ is the Rune of death, destruction, chaos, regeneration, ruin, and transformation. It is used to break down any barriers and a strong soul is required to control the wild and raging energies of this Rune. It is a powerful Rune that can be used to raise and control lightening and storms. Many of the great souls that inhabit the Otherworld were wild and strong in this world and have grown stronger in the Otherworld. There are other inhabitants in the Otherworld that are NOT known in our iteration. Weakness in the Otherworld is rewarded with defeat and sometimes the shredding and consuming of the soul – never to return in ANY iteration.

Eihwaz/Eoh ᛇ is the Rune associated with death and power over the dead. It is used to burn off the veil of forgetfulness from our soul, regaining the knowledge and powers gained from our prior lives. It is also used to shield our soul from hardships and attacks. As the seasons cycle and transform, our soul and journeys reflects this transformation through our multiple births and deaths in various dimensional universes and iterations.

Sowilo/Sól ᛋ is the Rune of the Sun, invincibility, and final triumph. It is the Rune of movement and bestows motivation upon the soul. Sowilo/Sól is used to shield the soul and project the magickal, attacking energies from the soul. It also provides insight and an understanding of the Otherworld. Sowilo/Sól energizes the Bind Rune, burning it into the soul.

Some we meet in the Otherworld can be hostile. The integrated energies of the Bind Rune provide a powerful tool for Otherworld travels. The physical manifestation of the Runes and Bind Runes can't be carried into the Otherworld, but they are emblazed on our soul. Not all are ready or willing to traverse the Otherworld. It's not a journey for the weak soul. Otherworld guides can help in your journeys until your soul has strengthened.

My Otherworld Journey in a Former Life

Two ravens glide overhead as I make my way through the misty, rubble strewn path. The corpses of dead trees stand as silent sentinels guarding the narrow rocky canyon pass. My soul feels the vibrational energies of an unseen threat. My heightened senses scream warnings of danger. Cautiously I push forward as the mists thicken. My sword, Fragarach leads the way.

Fragarach, the great retaliator, a gift obtained during a traversal in the Otherworld. None can lie with the point at their throat. Nothing can resist the cutting of the fine blade and NONE recover from a wound inflicted by it. The elements are controlled by its bearer. Fragarach can see the threat and communicates with my soul.

Suddenly, a headless, screaming wild woman appears between two of the trees. She grasps the trunks with her claw-like toe nails as she speaks magickal words in another language. Most of her rotting flesh has fallen from her bones and claws have replaced her finger nails. Her head with red glowing eyes is housed in her pelvis. She hisses as she strikes out with her long narrow tongue. As I dodge her attacks, her tongue rips the remaining bark from the trees beside me and crushes the rocks into powder.

"What do you seek besides death? Intruder!"

I answer with silence.

"Speak before I shred your soul!"

As I inch closer, I answer, "I have come to take your powers and extinguish your soul!"

With a great scream, her head launches from her pelvis. As the flaming red eyes and whipping tongue approach, I cleave the head and torso in half with Fragarach. Fragarach absorbs her energies, powers, and knowledge. I absorb them from Fragarach.

I turn and vanish from the Otherworld as I savor the new energies and powers. I thank Fragarach as I return him to his sheath. My entry into the Otherworld was through a deep pool at the edge of a large forest. Waiting for me is one of my enemies.

He commands, "Dark Druid! Show yourself!"

Once again, I answer with silence. Using my newly gained powers and knowledge, I launch fireballs at my enemy and his army, consuming them all.

Silently, I walk down the road past the smoldering flesh of men and beast to my home deep in a forested mountain side. My ravens, Odinsblood and Ashling glide silently overhead, ever watchful. I can see and hear what they see and hear. Transforming into a dark wulf, I race through the wooded trails, pursued by my companions. Upon my return, I'm greeted by a white wulf. After our homecoming frolic, we settle down to a quiet evening beside a whispering waterfall as we watch the fish leap at the low flying insects in the late afternoon sunlight.

Otherworld Travel from my book, *Mists of Dawn*

The Book of Thoth

Moraxthia slumped into a chair at the golden table. She began to sob as the impact of Melkatees' sacrifice registered. Thoth walked behind her and placed his hands on her soft shoulders. Waves of powerful energy flowed through Moraxthia as he spoke.

"Do not grieve for Melkatees. He willingly fulfilled the request of the dimensional universe. His love and confidence in your abilities were expressed in our conversations not long afterwards. Raythoriz also spoke very highly of your abilities and character. Ma'at has judged you in countless iterations and provides nothing but accolades for your character and abilities. I have recorded your iterations and know of your abilities and the purity of your soul."

After a pause he continued, "For these reasons, I offer you sacred knowledge and powers only a few have attained. Beware, you must remain pure in heart. Access to these powers and knowledge will test the very limits of your abilities. If you fail, you will be stripped of all your knowledge and powers and become as Melkatees. Neither able to help the other. Additionally, Nesfereta will loose his bonding with you and will be at the whims of this precarious situation. His fate will be determined by his and the remaining companion's ability to turn the loss. Do you accept these conditions?"

After a moment of reflection, Moraxthia affirmed her acceptance of the terms.

Placing his hands on her head, Thoth projected the images of a book with golden pages. The book was buried at the bottom of a river protected by his sacred guardians. A great city was located on the East bank of the river inhabited by more of Thoth's sacred guardians. He revealed the river and city was located in an ancient dimensional universe. Lastly, he imprinted an energy sample of the universe and iteration on Moraxthia's soul.

Taking her hand, he bid her to rise, "You must be anointed with the sacred oils if you are to survive the journey. Remove your clothing and stand before me."

Moraxthia hesitated, but removed her clothing. Thoth was entranced with her beauty as she stood naked in the soft candlelight. He had been the consort to many humanoids over multiple iterations.

Lifting a bottle of golden oil from the table he poured a small stream on Moraxthia's head. Speaking ancient words of power he caused the oil to ignite and fuse with her skin. Taking a second bottle, he dipped his finger in the oil and made sacred marks on Moraxthia's body. One on each breast, one above her navel, and one above her right knee. Thoth's touch energized and aroused her. When he rose, she noticed he was erect. This further aroused her.

He projected, "Reach for my staff and take me within. I can provide pleasure beyond anything you can imagine."

His words aroused her further. She unsheathed his phallus and began to stroke it. Contact with his erection caused intense, orgasmic energies to race through her body. She shuddered as her knees weakened. Her desire for Thoth swelled.

Faintly, she heard the dimensional universe whisper, "Moraxthia, remember your duties. If you copulate with Thoth, all will be lost."

Summoning her energies, Moraxthia dissipated her desires for Thoth. As if waking from a dream, she saw her reflection in a large pool as she stood beside him. He was enshrouded in golden, ornate robes and smiling at her. She was dressed in a dark, sleeveless gown with long, dark arm coverings. A dark cape with a pattern of golden intertwined knots around the edge was draped around her shoulders. Her head covering reflected the same golden pattern around its edge.

Thoth pointed to the pool and revealed, "This is the gateway to the river and the city where my book of gold is hidden. You have been clothed in body and soul with my sacred marks and colors. These identify you as an apprentice of Thoth."

Moraxthia was embarrassed to meet his gaze.

She declared, "I am not worthy of this honor."

"You have shown your integrity once again. I am honored to name you as my apprentice." He soothed.

"What of our interlude?" She sheepishly asked.

"All things are vibrational energy. Our energies intertwined for a short period at a higher level than your shield skin."

"Did we physically interact or was it a dream?" She questioned.

"It's all the same once you progress to a high enough level. It's an exchange of energies. I tested you to see if you would succumb to your desires. Sexual energies are the strongest vibrational energies in the dimensional universe."

"If I had taken you, what would have happened?" Moraxthia prodded.

"Your bonding with Nesfereta would have been broken and you would not have advanced to a grand master in this iteration," he disclosed.

"Would your bonding with Seshat have been broken?"

"No. We're bonded at a higher level and live under a higher dimensional law."

"You mean you can have as many sex partners or wives as you want?"

"That is an oversimplification, but in your terms that would be the closest answer I could give you. We exist in multiple iterations at the same time. Seshat and I have been bonded over all the iterations that we exist together. In other iterations where we don't exist together I am bonded with others. Seshat and I have progressed beyond great grand masters," Thoth tried to clarify.

"I don't completely understand," Moraxthia confessed.

"At this point you don't need to. As you progress it will become clear."

Turning to the pool Thoth instructed, "Project yourself into the pool and follow the energy imprints revealed to your soul. When you emerge, seek out the leader of my sacred guardians. Speak the words of power I have provided to subdue her. Persuade her to reveal the secrets of the depths and the guardians of my golden book. When you have obtained the book return here. DO NOT open or read the book until I have instructed you to do so. You are NOT ready for the sacred knowledge contained in the book. We have to prepare your soul and shield skin. I will watch your journey. I am only a witness of the outcome of your efforts for the dimensional universe. You must complete this task on your own."

Moraxthia turned while she sang a runic song of power Thoth had taught her. A great golden orb encircled her as she projected into the pool. Following the energy projections, she crossed multiple dimensional universes. She traveled for what seemed like eons of time finally reaching an ancient dimensional universe. It felt old, but powerful. She adjusted her soul and shield skin to its rhythms as Thoth had taught her. Melkatees had initially trained her to adjust her rhythms, but Thoth had taken her quantum magnitudes beyond his training.

As Moraxthia emerged on the banks of the river near the city gate, her golden orb dissipated. Her energy projections attracted the attention of Thoth's sacred guardians. Mammoth scorpions and poisonous snakes converged on Moraxthia. Singing a runic song of power, Moraxthia suspended the guardians in the air. Walking past them, she proceeded to the center of the city and what appeared to be the main palace. More guardians surrounded the palace. Shifting to her totem form, Moraxthia quickly bypassed the guardians and entered the palace.

Following the strongest energy projections, she reached a great hall in the center of the palace. Enshrouded in thin silk curtains was a raised platform. Aromatic incense exuded through the silk and drifted into the great hall. Pausing, Moraxthia transformed from her totem.

A deep voice greeted her, "Welcome daughter of Perd and novice of Thoth. Enter if you dare and speak your request."

Moraxthia slowly walk towards the platform and parted the veil. She hesitated for a moment as she appraised the leader of Thoth's sacred guardians.

"What were you expecting, a weak minded humanoid?" The leader challenged.

"No, but I wasn't expecting Ammut," she replied.

"I am NOT Ammut! I am her mother. You'd think the great Thoth, keeper of all knowledge, would educate his novices about the lineage of his more important guardians! The last novice that came here, Asteroid or something like that didn't have a clue either!" The indignant leader huffed.

Smiling, Moraxthia bowed as she corrected, "Her name was Astorath, noble leader."

"How am I to remember? He sends his novices here every thousand or so iterations for his golden book. They're always women, never men. Asteroid was here not too long ago, but I can barely remember her visit. She was lovely for a humanoid, but not as lovely as Seshat. You are a lovely one too, have you ridden his golden pony?" The leader leered as she watched Moraxthia's response.

Laughing, the leader soothed, "Don't look so shocked! It seems that's all men of any species think about!"

"I didn't come here to banter the sexual exploits of the races in the various iterations!" Moraxthia snapped.

"My, my, Thoth choose a spicy one this time. This should be interesting," the leader retorted.

After a further pause the leader questioned Moraxthia, "Why have you journeyed here?"

"Thoth commanded that I obtain his golden book."

"What do you know of the book?" The leader questioned.

"Very little except it is made of gold."

"Is it the gold you want?"

"No, the knowledge and power it contains."

"I have never seen the book, but I can tell you where it is hidden and what guards it. In exchange for this information I require a favor, an errand," the leader revealed.

"What is your request?" Moraxthia asked.

"I have an enemy I wish you to kill."

"Make another request!"

"I wish you to steal two valuable books from another enemy."

"I won't! Give me a request that I can grant!"

"I want your child when she is born."

In a rage Moraxthia rebuked the leader, "I would never hand my child over! If you won't make a reasonable request I will discover the location of Thoth's book myself!"

"Even if you could locate it, you couldn't get past the guardians without the passwords. Even with the passwords you'll have to battle the guardians once you take the golden book. Without the passwords you'll never have a chance to obtain the book."

After a pause, the leader continued, "Even though your child would be delicious, I would rather have a fine meal with my daughter, Ammut. I haven't eaten with her in years. That is my price, convince Ammut to dine with me tonight and I will show you where Thoth's golden book is located and provide you with the passwords. The rest will be up to you."

"That is all you require?"

"Yes."

"Ammut is with one of my companions. They were tasked by Thoth to capture and return our adversary, Jakathorb."

"Jakathorb!" The leader snapped.

"You know him?" Moraxthia asked.

"Know him! Know him! That little thief and trickster stole some magickal items presented to me by Thoth! If I ever get my jaws on him…bring him to dinner as well! He'll taste bad, but I'll wash his taste away with strong drink…that weasel! You do know that Jakathorb was Thoth's apprentice? What a tragedy."

Moraxthia was shocked at the revelation, although it did explain the advanced abilities that Jakathorb had exhibited.

She negotiated, "I will return with Ammut, but I can't return with Jakathorb. Thoth has commanded Jakathorb was to be returned unharmed so they could converse."

The leader countered, "If there is anything left of Jakathorb after Thoth has talked to that weasel I want you to bring him here. I will settle for that and dinner with my daughter, Ammut."

"I agree to your terms," Moraxthia replied.

Shifting to her totem form, she raced from the palace returning to the water's edge. Moraxthia transformed from her totem form and sang a runic song of power recreating the golden orb. Projecting into the water, Moraxthia followed her energy trail back to the terrace.

Quietly, Moraxthia entered the hall of Roxthanea and her companions. Sekhmet was in her predatory form. Ammut and Sekhmet had Roxthanea cornered as they paced dangerously close. Moraxthia spoke words of power and emitted violet bolts of energy from her palms that immobilized the pair.

Startled, Roxthanea shouted, "Don't hurt them! We're training!"

Moraxthia released the pair and apologized.

The shock had transformed Sekhmet from her predatory form.

Angry she replied, "Are you always sneaking around and attacking people?"

"No, that was not my intent. I thought you two were finishing what you started earlier."

Ammut joined in, "I see Thoth has wasted no time in advancing your training. What else has he taught you?"

Ignoring Ammut's suggestive remark, she addressed Roxthanea, "I would request that you allow Ammut to accompany me on an errand for Thoth. I will only need her services for the evening."

"We were to leave shortly to fulfill our mission for Thoth," Roxthanea protested.

"If you can delay until midnight, I will return with Ammut and I will provide magick you can use in your quest for Jakathorb," Moraxthia promised.

Sekhmet intervened, "Spend time with me great wulf and protector of Alzada. I can teach you many things about battle while we wait."

After a moment of reflection, Roxthanea agreed providing they returned by midnight. The two new companions exited the hall and walked to the edge of the pool.

Ammut questioned, "Do you know where this leads? How did you discover this passageway?"

"It leads to many places, but we're traveling to an ancient dimensional universe. We're going to dine with your mother."

"Are you insane! My mother will have both of us for dinner!"

"Not if I can help it!"

"Great! I have to put my life in your hands! You're not even a grand master and Thoth hasn't had time…oh never mind! Let's go to dinner with my mother."

Moraxthia once again sang a runic song of power creating a golden glowing orb around them and projected into the pool. Following the energy projections Thoth had provided, she once again reached the iteration of Ammut's mother.

The sacred guardians had reinforcements this time. Crocodiles projected immense waves of energy at the pair. Ammut uttered a single word of power that extinguished the energy waves and shrank the crocodiles. She giggled as she slurped up the morsels.

"I just love appetizers!"

Moraxthia shook her head as she walked into the palace. The other sacred guardians were reluctant to engage the pair. Without further incident they entered the central chamber, but it was empty.

"This is not good!" Warned Ammut.

From the depths of the room, Ammut's mother rushed forward. Her front claws lashed out at Moraxthia as her snout closed just inches away from her daughter.

Moraxthia shouted the words of power that Thoth had revealed to her. Ammut's mother became rigid and ceased her attacks. Ammut turned to Moraxthia with a surprised look.

"What did you do?"

"Thoth gave me words of power to subdue your mother."

"What else did Thoth give you?" She asked suggestively.

Moraxthia turned to Ammut's mother and declared, "I can release you and we can have a nice dinner together OR I can leave you to watch us enjoy our dinner. In either case, you WILL provide the information I need to recover Thoth's golden book when we are done OR I will show you other things I have learned from Thoth!"

Her mother agreed to her terms if Moraxthia would release her.

Ammut was uncomfortable with the arrangement.

"I don't think it is wise to release her."

"Won't she honor her agreement?"

"Not if she can find a way around it. It is the nature of our kind."

"To act dishonorably?"

"No. We seek an advantage over our adversary through weakness."

"Thoth provided me with words of power and her secret name!" Moraxthia informed them both.

She warned Ammut, "Remember, the dimensional universe provided me with your secret name."

"Yes, I remember."

Ammut turned to her mother, "It seems we'll have to enjoy the company of this mortal for the evening. Let's declare a truce and enjoy the evening."

Her mother nodded in agreement. Moraxthia released her mother and sat at a large table near the fire. The other two companions joined her. Servants entered the room with large platters of meat and tankards of strong drink.

The trio feasted as they exchanged tales of their adventures. Moraxthia noticed the strong drink rapidly affected the mother and daughter causing them to become more agreeable and relaxed.

After they had finished dinner and their tales of adventure, Moraxthia rose and bid the mother to reveal the location of Thoth's golden book and the passwords.

Staggering from her chair, she walked out the door and down a long passage to the river's edge. Moraxthia and Ammut followed.

Pointing down the river to a partially submerged structure, she proclaimed, "In the bowels of the shrine you will find Thoth's golden book. Beware, it is protected by all manner of sacred guardians. The passwords will allow passage into the shrine. When you remove the book the passwords will not appease the sacred guardians. You will have to rely on your own abilities to leave with Thoth's golden book. We'll wait here and witness your fate."

Evoking words of power, Moraxthia vibrated the rune ᚠ, Fé. While the energies still lingered, she vibrated the rune ᚭ, Óss. She parted the waters to the shrine using the energies from the vibrations of the rune ᚦ, Þurs. Vibrating the rune ᛁ, Íss Moraxthia froze the waters creating a path to the shrine. Vibrating the rune ᚲ, Kaun Moraxthia illuminated the path and the interior of the building.

Gliding down the path, she noticed a number of sacred guardians suspended in the frozen waters. The shrine still contained a large number of guardians unaffected by her magick. A massive pair of guardians blocked her way as she reached the steps.

"Who dares to enter the shrine of Thoth?" One of them challenged.

"The daughter of Perd and novice of Thoth. Thoth has commanded that I retrieve his golden book," Moraxthia replied.

Suspicious, the other guardian challenged, "Over the eons, there have been many attempts to steal the sacred text. What proof do you have of your commission?"

Forming the correct sequence of signs, Moraxthia uttered the passwords to accompany them.

"Your magickal abilities are impressive, daughter of Perd. You may pass," the guardians replied as they bowed.

Moraxthia heard the dimensional universe whisper, Follow the lighted path to the lowest level. The Book of Thoth lies there.

As she passed through the multiple corridors to the lowest level of the shrine she could feel the energies of the unseen guardians lurking in the shadows. After passing through dozens of levels, she reached the chamber containing the Book of Thoth. She could feel its energies, but she couldn't see it. In the middle of the room was a podium with an iron box. Intermeshed with the box were poisonous snakes, spiders, and scorpions. Encircled around the box was a colossal serpent.

"Who dares to disturb the sacred Book of Thoth?" The serpent challenged.

"The daughter of Perd and novice of Thoth. Thoth has commanded that I retrieve his golden book," Moraxthia once again replied.

"What proof of your words do you provide?" He further challenged uncoiling from the iron box and moving towards Moraxthia.

"Examine my robes, shield skin, and soul. You will find the marks of a grand master and of Thoth."

As she started to speak the passwords and form the signs, the serpent laughed and chided her.

"Your magick doesn't work here. I can't be killed or manipulated like the other guardians. Thoth has enhanced my soul beyond any magick of the dimensional universe."

Sampling the energies of the lower chamber and the energies of the next level, Moraxthia concluded his claim was only valid for this chamber.

The serpent continued, "Even if you could get past me, you still have to contend with the guardians encrusted in the iron box. Assuming you somehow got past them, how will you pass all the other guardians as you ascend through the multiple levels to the surface? You will have to contend with physical guardians and magickal traps! How does a mere humanoid with a few words of magick and some archaic passwords deal with the overwhelming forces of Thoth?"

He concluded, "My advice is to return to Thoth and report your failure."

Striking out at Moraxthia the guardian contacted her flesh and injected his poison. Moraxthia reeled back and dropped to her knees as waves of magick and poison raced through her shield skin and soul. The serpent moved closer to strike again and finish Thoth's novice.

Summoning her energies, Moraxthia vibrated the runes Þ, Þurs and I, Íss as she projected their energies at the serpent. The serpent was immobilized. The effort had drained most of her remaining energies. Connecting to the infinite energies of the dimensional universe, she vibrated the rune ᛚ, Lögur driving the poisons from her body and restoring her strength.

Approaching the immobilized serpent, she replied, "Perhaps your enhancements shield you from less advanced magickal users. I have progressed to levels most can't comprehend. I may not be able to kill you, but you will remain immobilized until I have completed my tasking."

"Not since the last magickal user, Jakathorb who appeared hundreds of iterations ago have I encountered a novice as powerful. Before Jakathorb, it was Astorath. She was preceded by Seshat."

Moraxthia questioned him, "What can you tell me about Jakathorb?"

"He was the first male novice Thoth had taken. He was very talented, but his heart wasn't pure. If one with an impure heart reads the secrets contained in Thoth's book it will either kill them or corrupt them further. Thoth tried to purify his apprentice, but the book corrupted him. In the end, Jakathorb tried to take control of this dimension until his masters appeared. Thoth had summoned them to return Jakathorb to their care. It took Thoth, Ammut's mother, and his three masters to subdue Jakathorb. Thoth tried to remove all the knowledge of the book from Jakathorb's soul, but some things can't be removed. Thoth covered those things that couldn't be removed with a protective layer of pain. If Jakathorb tries to access this knowledge directly or indirectly, his shield skin and soul are thrashed with unbearable pain. At one point, Jakathorb will burn off this veil of pain and pose a threat to us all. Beware, you must remain pure of heart if you partake of this knowledge."

After a moment of reflection Moraxthia proposed, "You seem docile enough and have been very helpful. If I release your binding will you allow me to fulfill my master's decree?"

"I can not! I am bound to prevent the weak from taking the book. If you release me I will do all in my power to prevent you from taking the book!"

Moraxthia turned and walked near the book. The encrusted guardians followed her movements, ready to attack. She didn't know if more guardians or other traps were inside the iron box. She'd find out later when she returned the box to Thoth.

Sampling the energies of the iron box and the guardians, she detected additional boxes inside. She also felt the distinct energies of Thoth's golden book. Using words of power, Moraxthia caused the vibrational energies of the guardians to shift into another dimensional universe. Quickly, she snapped up the iron box and projected herself into the ethereal. As she projected, the energies that held the guardians in the other dimensional universe dissipated. Restored to their original dimension, they projected into the ethereal in pursuit of Moraxthia.

Using words of power, she combined the energies of ᚾ, Naud and ᛋ, Sól, creating an impenetrable barrier of fire. Vibrating the rune ᚲ, Kaun Moraxthia projected the inferno at the guardians.

Sensing the futility of their situation, the guardians returned to the shrine to coordinate their efforts with the other guardians. Moraxthia followed her energy projections towards the terrace.

Suddenly the ethereal was filled with a host of guardians. Ammut's mother stepped forward and demanded that she hand over Thoth's golden book. Ammut accompanied her, eager to consume Moraxthia at her mother's command.

"I will NOT be swayed from my mission and I will NOT tolerate your interference. Move aside and take your army with you or suffer the consequences!" Moraxthia warned.

Ammut leaped forward snapping at Moraxthia. Moraxthia spoke Thoth's words of power and Ammut's secret name binding her. Ammut's mother lunged forward along with Thoth's guardians. Using Thoth's words of power and the mother's secret name, Moraxthia bound her too. Vibrating the runes ᚾ, Hagall and ᚦ, Þurs Moraxthia combined them with the rune ᚤ, Ár and created a swirling vortex that subdued the guardians. Vibrating the rune ᚱ, Reið she transported the subdued guardians back to the shrine.

Addressing Ammut's mother, "I will return to Thoth with his golden book and your daughter. I will leave you to return to your world. Know I have not stolen the Book of Thoth and I will provide him with a positive report of your efforts and the other guardians to protect it. I'm sure we'll meet again as adversaries and I don't begrudge your efforts. Your binding will not release until Ammut, Thoth's book, and I have reached our sanctuary."

Moraxthia turned and projected into the waters with Ammut in tow. Reaching the terrace she released Ammut from her binding.

"Please follow me so I can keep our appointment with Roxthanea."

Ammut grunted and followed.

Allen Hartley

Stairway To Heaven

There's a lady who's sure all that glitters is gold
And she's buying a stairway to heaven
When she gets there she knows, if the stores are all closed
With a word she can get what she came for
And she's buying a stairway to heaven

There's a sign on the wall but she wants to be sure
'Cause you know sometimes words have two meanings
In a tree by the brook, there's a songbird who sings
Sometimes all of our thoughts are misgiven...

There's a feeling I get when I look to the west
And my spirit is crying for leaving
In my thoughts I have seen rings of smoke through the trees
And the voices of those who stand looking...

And it's whispered that soon if we all call the tune
Then the piper will lead us to reason
And a new day will dawn for those who stand long
And the forests will echo with laughter

If there's a bustle in your hedgerow, don't be alarmed now
It's just a spring clean for the May queen
Yes, there are two paths you can go by, but in the long run
There's still time to change the road you're on
And it makes me wonder

Your head is humming and it won't go, in case you don't know
The piper's calling you to join him
Dear lady, can you hear the wind blow and did you know
Your stairway lies on the whispering wind?

And as we wind on down the road
Our shadows taller than our soul
There walks a lady we all know
Who shines white light and wants to show
How everything still turns to gold

And if you listen very hard
The tune will come to you at last
When all are one and one is all…

And she's buying a stairway to heaven…

Led Zeppelin

Allen Hartley

Chapter 4
The Soul

My soul's fibers had become rigid and encrusted as a result of the unbalanced path I had followed. When I was younger, I listened to my soul and heeded its quiet messages. Ignoring these promptings often resulted in missed opportunities and misfortune. Some of these promptings were from my past lives trying to convey knowledge and wisdom. Others were from the dimensional universe. As life progressed, I listened to them less often. Logic and new directions encouraged by others drowned out these quiet messages. The new, louder voices came from religious leaders, peers, friends, family, society, and most especially, my former spouse. It reminds me of the song by Sting, "DeDoDo"-

Poets priests and politicians
Have words to thank for their positions
Words that scream for your submission...

Cause when their eloquence escapes you
Their logic ties you up and rapes you...

In our current iteration, a veil of forgetfulness has been placed over our souls. Those that are strong enough will burn the veil off and reclaim the powers and knowledge from their former lives/iterations. In the early 1990's, I had the realization of the need to reclaim my soul and make a major course correction. It would be a long and difficult journey, one that I would make alone. It would require the severance of all ties binding me to the current unbalanced path. This struggle was filled with many years of failures before I was strong enough to move forward and not constantly look back. You can't move forward when you're looking backward. It was during this time my soul made a journey to the Otherworld. It took weeks, but in February 1996, my former spouse created the situation that allowed me to shatter the rigid fibers of my soul that bound me to an unbalanced path. She had expected a different result that would have benefited her immensely, materially and financially. That journey changed my perspective on many things. During this journey I made significant progress burning off the veil of forgetfulness and adjusting my course. I had many things to unlearn and reorient. Until a person has experienced an Otherworld journey, they can't understand how unbalanced they are. I will spend the rest of this life building from these experiences.

Your soul is ancient and eternal; it weaves you into the great tapestry of spirit that connects everything everywhere.

Four Elements

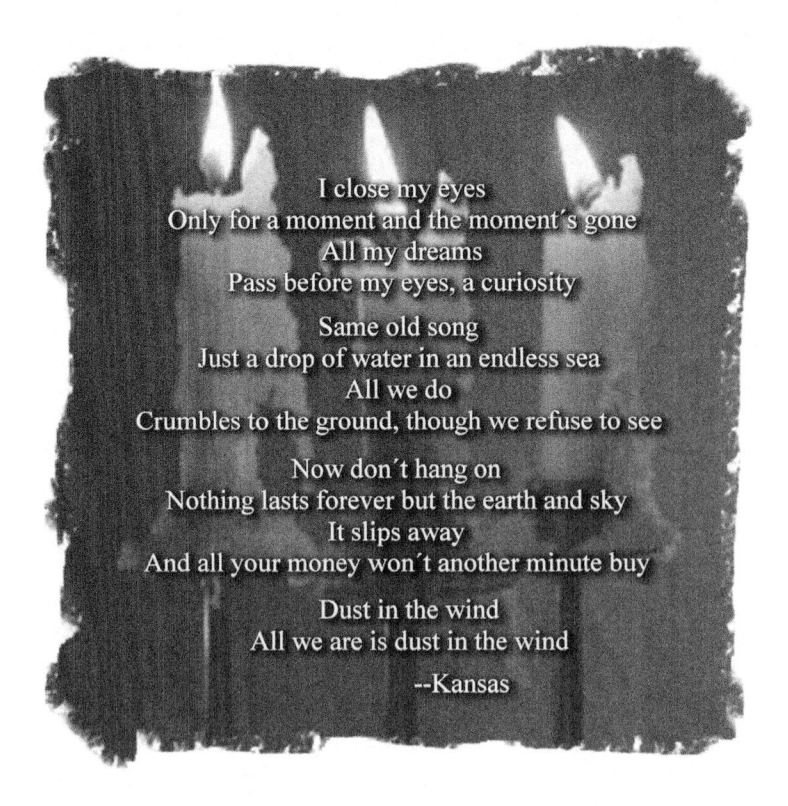

I close my eyes
Only for a moment and the moment's gone
All my dreams
Pass before my eyes, a curiosity

Same old song
Just a drop of water in an endless sea
All we do
Crumbles to the ground, though we refuse to see

Now don't hang on
Nothing lasts forever but the earth and sky
It slips away
And all your money won't another minute buy

Dust in the wind
All we are is dust in the wind

--Kansas

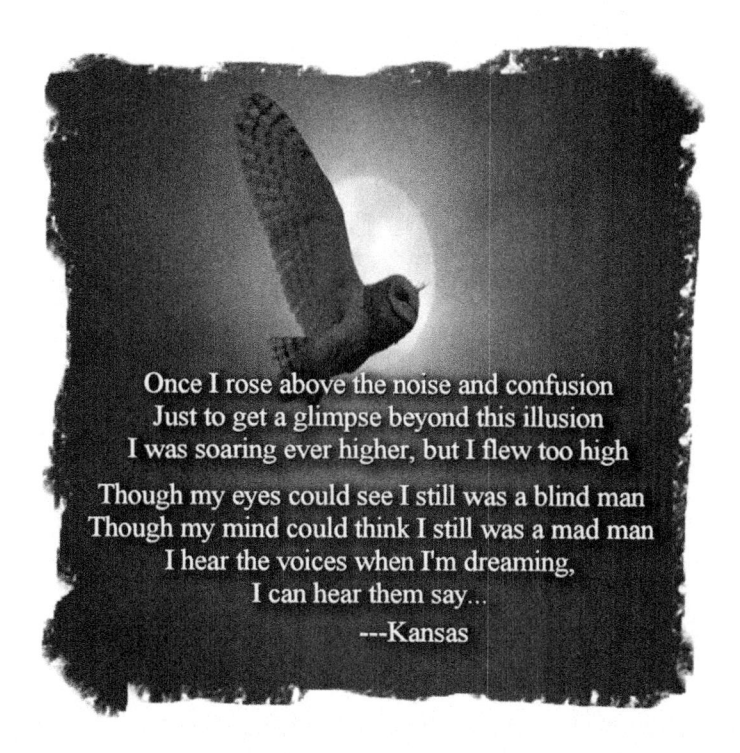

> Once I rose above the noise and confusion
> Just to get a glimpse beyond this illusion
> I was soaring ever higher, but I flew too high
>
> Though my eyes could see I still was a blind man
> Though my mind could think I still was a mad man
> I hear the voices when I'm dreaming,
> I can hear them say...
> ---Kansas

What is the soul? It is the composition of all your knowledge, powers, and projected will accumulated over multiple iterations/lives. Not just your knowledge, powers, and projected will, but also those of your ancestors. Contrary to what many proclaim, this is NOT the first life we have lived in this dimensional universe. We have returned multiple times to this and other iterations. Our ancestors pass to us our names, blood, and the collective knowledge, powers, and projected will of our family lines. Our current iteration/lifetime is the most challenging. We must carefully listen to our souls to discover who we are, what our true path is, and how to recover our former knowledge and powers. Our current society has been so polluted and corrupted that only the strong will prevail. Sadly, that number will not be large.

One of the most corrupt practices encouraged by our society is the pollution and mixing of the blood lines. Especially, the mixing of the cursed lines with the pure lines. In addition to polluting the blood lines, our TRUE history, heritage, and minds are being polluted through distortions, revisions, and propaganda. These intense efforts are facilitated through religion, society, media, and the politically correct propaganda mongers.

Blood is one of the most ancient and wisest streams in the universe. It is the stream of ancestry. An ancient bloodline flows from the past generations until it reaches and creates us now. Blood holds and carries life. From mythic times, blood has been at the heart of sacrifice; life was offered both as plea and praise to the deities.

Except for our parents and grandparents, our ancestors have vanished. Yet ultimately and proximately, it is the ancestors who call us here. We belong to their lifeline. While they ground our unknown memory, our continuity bestows on them a certain oblique eternity. In our presence we entwine past and future.

Eternal Echoes

We are so inundated with the distractions of careers, the acquisition of "things", disasters, societal guilt, status and image, wealth, control of others, media, and religion that we have little or no time to discover who we really are. We have even less time to hear the soft whisperings of our soul and the dimensional universe.

AS WE JOURNEY from the womb of the sea with our gaze of longing fixed on the stars, we have stopped off on this earth for a short spell of belonging. The unity of the four elements is what constitutes and sustains our existence in this world.

Four Elements

In the Celtic tradition there is a fascinating interflow between soul and matter and between time and eternity. This rhythm also includes and engages the human body. The human body is a mirror and expression of the world of soul.

Anam Cara: A Book of Celtic Wisdom

Our soul, joined with our physical body is the manifestation of the unity of the four elements with the soul – the fifth element. Our flesh was created from the element of earth and filled with the element of water. The fire within us ignites the energies allowing our organs, brain, and neuronic pathways to operate. The air we inhale feeds the internal fires. Our soul is united with the flesh as long as the flesh remains pure enough to support it. When it isn't, our soul departs through the gateway of death and returns to the Otherworld to prepare for the next life/iteration. All the knowledge and powers we have gained in this life and uncovered from previous lives remains with our souls. Knowledge and powers that haven't been uncovered are restored when we leave the veil for forgetfulness at the doorway of death.

Traditionally, the breath was understood as the pathway through which the soul entered the body. Breaths come in pairs except the first breath and the last breath. At the deepest level, breath is sister of spirit.

Anam Cara: A Book of Celtic Wisdom

"All things share the same breath— the beast, the tree, the man ... the air shares its spirit with all the life it supports."

Chief Seattle

Nine Runes represent the union of the elements and soul. Combining the Runes representing the elements into Bind Runes, produces a five pointed star arrangement. The soul is represented by the Rune, ᛉ Algiz/Eolh. Its position at the bottom of the inverted star represents the intake of the energies from the four elements and dimensional universe. Just as a funnel channels a broad path of inbound items into a focused output, the inverted star represents the same concept. This is the correct position of the star to allow the soul to receive the energies of the dimensional universe.

The top left position of the inverted star is the element of fire. This Bind Rune was created from the two Runes, ᛋ Sowilo/Sól and ᛇ Eihwaz/Eoh.

Sowilo/Sól is the Rune of the Sun. It also symbolizes the lightning bolt and spark of life. Without these energies, all things would cease to exist.

Eihwaz/Eoh is the Rune of transformation through death and rebirth. It shields the soul through all manner of hardship and can be used to gain knowledge and powers from our former lives.

The combined Runes produce the Bind Rune ᛔ Bercna/Bjarkan. Bercna/Bjarkan represents new beginnings, birth, and growth. It is the feminine Rune of nurturing and magick. The three Runes tie together the concepts of the eternal cycles of our physical bodies and souls. We also see the same cycles reflected in the seasons of our world.

We have falsely spatialized the eternal world. We have driven the eternal out into some kind of distant galaxy. Yet the eternal world does not seem to be a place but rather a different state of being. The soul of the person goes no place because there is no place else to go. This suggests that the dead are here with us, in the air that we are moving through all the time. The only difference between us and the dead is that they are now in an invisible form. You cannot see them with the human eye. But you can sense the presence of those you love who have died. With the refinement of your soul, you can sense them. You feel that they are near.

Anam Cara: A Book of Celtic Wisdom

The top right position of the inverted star is the element of air. This Bind Rune was created from the two Runes, ᛕ Perthro/Perð and ᚲ Kenaz/Kaun.

Perthro/Perð is the Rune of divination and meditation. It is used to reclaim lost knowledge and wisdom not only of the Runes, but our past lives and that of our ancestors.

Kenaz/Kaun is the Rune of illumination and penetration. It is used to illuminate the soul, providing awareness and insight.

The Bind Rune composed from these two Runes allows the soul to discover and comprehend all that is hidden. The hidden plans of an enemy, knowledge of our past lives and ancestors, or the knowledge of the dimensional universe.

The world of thought resides in the air. All of our thoughts happen in the air element. Our greatest thoughts come to us from the generosity of the air. It is here that the idea of inspiration is rooted. You inspire or breathe in the thoughts concealed in the air element.

Anam Cara: A Book of Celtic Wisdom

The bottom left position of the inverted star represents the element of earth. The Bind Rune for this position was created from the combined Runes ᛖ Ehwaz/Eykur and ᛚ Lagus/Lögur.

Ehwaz/Eykur represents the horse which is one of the sacred animals. It also forges bonds between souls and seals relationships.

Lagus/Lögur is used to enhance physical and magickal strength. It reveals the unknown, helping us to be aware of the energies around us, making us more sensitive to the messages and knowledge sent to our souls from our past lives and the dimensional universe.

The Bind Rune formed from these two is ᛖ. Another aspect of Lagus/Lögur is revealed from this Bind Rune. Lagus/Lögur not only reveals the unknown, but it can be used to conceal the unknown just as it conceals itself in the Bind Rune.

"A soul's outcome in the afterlife is based on knowledge."
Thoth

Not all souls are ready or want to discover and contemplate their past lives, knowledge, and powers. There are many that encourage weakness and laziness by not doing anything or turning their lives over to someone else to manage. We are here in these iterations to strengthen and advance our souls with knowledge and power. It is our responsibility to advance and progress. Our future will depend on how we advance ourselves in this iteration.

The bottom right position of the inverted star represents the element of water. This Bind Rune is formed from the two Runes, ᚾ Nauthiz/Nauð and ᚹ Wunjo/Vin.

Nauthiz/Nauð Represents the dark night of the soul. It is the Rune of endurance and will, to carry on when all hope seems lost. Like the element of water, the situation under the influence of Nauthiz/Nauð is very tenuous at best.

Wunjo/Vin is the Rune of honors and rewards. It is also the Rune of healing. After successfully working through the trials and testing of the Nauthiz/Nauð Rune, the soul will need the soothing energies from Wunjo/Vin.

The Bind Rune produced from the merging of these two is ᚦ Thurisaz/þurs. This is the Rune of destructive power, chaos, and ruin. It also symbolizes death and regeneration, transformation, and the breaking down of barriers. From these come wisdom, courage, physical strength, independence, and leadership. Those that survive are made stronger and the weak are culled. It is the natural way of the universe.

Chapter 5
Ancestry

Our ancestors pass to us our blood, name, knowledge, gifts, and magick. It is our responsibility to pass these things to our descendents with honor and enrichments. In reality, there are those that would pollute and mix the bloodlines, names, knowledge, gifts, and magick in order to gain control over them. If they're successful, this can disrupt multiple generations until one is sent that is strong enough to restore them.

These ancestral gifts are passed genetically and through endowments to the soul. Since we have and will exist through multiple iterations in this dimensional universe, we pass these ancestral gifts to ourselves at various times. Once defiled, the name and blood are the most difficult to reclaim. Of the two, the name will be easiest to restore. Through powerful magick, many things can be rectified although, it is far better not to walk down the path that pollutes these ancestral gifts. Even with powerful magick, it may take generations to restore the name and even longer to restore the bloodline.

Adding honor to the family name and enhancing the other gifts passed to their descendents has always been a challenge.

Countless volumes have been recorded of the events that shaped our ancestors. For the astute, these records can guide them in their journey through the multiple iterations. Those that fail to study the past are doomed to repeat the same mistakes that ensnared our ancestors, some with dire consequences that will handicap multiple generations.

The Bind Rune for ancestry is created from eight Runes. These Runes are associated with a particular aspect of ancestry. When a Bind Rune is created, new Runes and meanings are derived from the merger. In this case, the Bind Rune for ancestry speaks of the future generations. The three obvious Runes are Tiwaz/Týr ↑, Ingwaz/Ing ◇, and Dagaz/Dagur ᛞ. In a pictorial interpretation of this Bind Rune, Tiwaz/Týr ↑ is representative of the phallus and Ingwaz/Ing ◇ the male seed sack. Dagaz/Dagur ᛞ represents the womb. The union of these produces the elements and spark of life that creates the next generation. All that has been and will be are contained in this Bind Rune pictorially and literally.

The base Rune used to create the Bind Rune for ancestry is Dagaz/Dagur ᛞ. Dagaz/Dagur provides the intuition and knowledge to understand our past lives and those of our ancestors.

It allows us to uncover the ancestral knowledge, gifts, and magickal powers that have been passed through our lineage. For many, the pollution of these ancestral gifts has to be removed before they can be fully realized. Knowledge and action are the basis of real power, while ignorance and laziness are the basis for losing power.

Othala/Óðal ᛉ is the traditional Rune of ancestry and heritage. Combined with Dagaz/Dagur, Othala/Óðal is used to discover our past lives, knowledge, magickal powers, ancestors, and the gifts of our ancestral pool. Just as property, possessions, titles, money, and other physical items can be passed from an ancestor to a descendent, there are items that are passed from the Otherworld ancestral collections. These are passed genetically and through endowments to the soul.

As above, so below; as below, so above.

The Kybalion.

Kenaz/Kaun ᚲ is the Rune associated with light of the soul and intellect. It is used as a guiding light in Otherworld travels and to illuminate the path to our ancestors. Kenaz/Kaun can penetrate and illuminate things which are veiled or hidden, especially to discover the ancestral gifts that have been passed to us. Many times, family names have been mottled when historical and legal records have been modified. Additionally, the other ancestral gifts may have been corrupted. Kenaz/Kaun can help us discover the true nature of these ancestral gifts.

Laguz/Lögur ᛚ is used to reveal the hidden or unknown. Combined with Kenaz/Kaun, Laguz/Lögur can help us probe deeper into our past lives and those of our ancestors. Laguz/Lögur can assist us in gaining a deeper understanding of the ancestral gifts that have been passed to us.

Ansuz/Óss ᚨ is power through speech. Using Ansuz/Óss, we can discover and converse with our ancestors. It can also be magickly used with Laguz/Lögur to reveal the hidden and bring order and clarity to our ancestral gifts, including the purification of the ancestral name and blood. Ansuz/Óss is a powerful Rune used to communicate with the Otherworld and converting your thoughts and will into actions.

Wunjo/Vin ᚹ is the Rune of rewards and honor. It is used to bring honor to the family name and to enhance the pool of ancestral gifts. Additionally, Wunjo/Vin can be used to unite families. It is also used to heal the soul and the physical body.

Raidho/Reið ᚱ represents travel and journeys. It represents our journey through multiple lives and dimensional universes. It also reflects the journeys of our ancestors. In addition, Raidho/Reið represents the quest of the unknown; the quest to discover our past lives, ancestral gifts and ancestors.

Jera/Ár ᛃ is the Rune of cycles; cycles of our multiple lives, ancestors, and ancestral gifts. Just as warriors return with battle damage, our ancestral gifts can at times be returned with damage from their traversal through an iteration. It should be the goal to return these ancestral gifts untarnished and enhanced. To do so requires one to discover and utilize them early in their life. In reality, there are those that seek to enslave us through the destruction of our heritage, unjustified guilt and shame, discouraging the discovery of who we really are and what we capable of achieving, pollution of our blood and ancestral gifts through race mixing, and the homogenizing and degradation of society. All these things tarnish and diminish our ancestral gifts.

One of the great traditions that celebrate our ancestors is Samhain. Samhain is a very magical time of the year. The people who follow the original ways of honoring the cycles of nature see Samhain as a time of death. It is a window through the veils of reality from this world to the next. In celebrating Samhain, we consciously dance, play, honor and ritually celebrate our connection to the Otherworld and our ancestors. Although some may think otherwise, we are surrounded by spirits, ancestors and light beings that are happy when we acknowledge their existence. In doing so, we add deeper meaning and connection to our lives. We don't have to struggle away on our own; we are supported in so many ways. Samhain is about opening and allowing that support to flow. As we show up and honor the spirit world they make their presence known in our lives.

Traditionally, Samhain is celebrated from sunset October 31 until sunset on November 1st. It is a Celtic festival that marks the end of the harvest season and the beginning of winter. It falls halfway between the autumn equinox and the winter solstice.

The Celtic mind was not burdened by dualism. It did not separate what belongs together. The Celtic imagination articulates the inner friendship that embraces Nature, divinity, underworld, and human world as one. The dualism that separates the visible from the invisible, time from eternity, the human from the divine, was totally alien to them.

Anam Cara: A Book of Celtic Wisdom

To illustrate the concepts of ancestry, the Otherworld, heritage, and ancestral gifts, I created the following short story using historical fiction.

McKenna's Gift

It was late evening when Luthias Black arrived at the hospital to see his newly arrived granddaughter. He'd driven for three days to North Idaho from Texas with only a few hours of sleep each day. On the last leg of his journey he'd checked into a motel for a nap and a shower. He resumed his journey dressed in the regimental Kilt of the Black Clan. It was a great honor to have a child to continue the Black lineage. For generations, the Black Clan produced pipers that led the Scottish warriors into battle. After the Battle of Culloden, one of the Black pipers was convicted of treason and executed. It was a hard time for the Scottish people, especially the Highlanders after the Jacobite uprising. The English enforced strict bans on possessing weapons, speaking the Gaelic language, wearing kilts or anything associated with the regimental dress of the Clans. They attempted to eliminate the Clan Chiefs and the pipers who rallied and led the Clans into battle. The only station higher than the piper was the Clan Chief.

As a young man, Luthias had piped his unit into battle, during Operation Epsom in WWII. The piper carried no weapons, only his bagpipes. Dressed in the regimental kilt of the Black Clan, ignoring the swarm of angry bullets, he led his unit across mine fields, barbed wire, trenches, and poison gas. The mortality rate was high for the pipers, but he continued the tradition of his ancestors. The Germans called the pipers "the screaming ladies from Hell."

Luthias met his deceased wife, Keeley while performing at the Great Highland games in the fall. She was a young Irish nurse that was serving at the local military hospital. As they shared the day, Luthias discovered Keeley was a second generation Irish American. Her family remained strong in their ancestor's pre-Christian traditions even though they had converted to Christianity centuries ago. Luthias still held to his family's pre-Christian beliefs and refused to convert. Conversion was the yoke of bondage and submission to the Protestant kings of Britain. His ancestors had paid with their blood, lands, language, and heritage because they refused to recognize the foreign monarch of Britain that slaughtered or enslaved those who wouldn't submit. His people were proud and strong. For hundreds of years they had repelled the Nordic, Saxon, and British invaders. Embracing any form of Christianity required the yoke of bondage and submission not only to the church, but a ruler backed by the church. It was the ultimate betrayal of his ancestors and people.

After the war, Luthias decided to visit Keeley at her Texas home. Keeley's family embraced Luthias as a son even though they had some discomfort about his fiery ways. Keeley was just as fiery and strong willed. She wasn't intimidated by Luthias. After all, as a young single woman, she had traveled half a world away to work in a military hospital. She helped the dying to bravely embrace death, comforted and cared for those who had lost limbs, assisted the surgeons with their efforts to salvage the war torn soldiers, and traveled to Ireland to embrace the land of her ancestors.

As time passed, Keeley and Luthias married. Luthias was granted dual citizenship and the couple started their family. Luthias found the Scottish and Irish communities in Texas had very few links to each other and even fewer links to their overseas relatives. The third and forth generation children born in America had little to no knowledge of their heritage. Some was by design and other was through neglect. Luthias decided to address the problem by organizing the Highland Games. These events included music, food, stories, apparel, and competitions from his Scottish homeland. As the Highland Games progressed, Luthias included the Irish communities in the games. It was a great time for all.

In addition to organizing the games, Luthias and Keeley established a chain of Celtic Heritage Centers that taught Gaelic languages, Scottish and Irish history, music, dance, pre-Christian beliefs, weaving and spinning, and anything else connected to their heritage. The most popular, but difficult lessons were the piping schools. Many wanted to play the Great Highland bagpipes, but it was a lifelong commitment and challenge. Luthias was the head of the piping schools and recruited pipers from the regiments of his homeland to be guest instructors each year. Some stayed for many years.

Sadly, Keeley had passed through the portals of death a few years ago and wouldn't be here physically to embrace their new granddaughter. He could feel her soul, it was always near, waiting for his journey through the same portals and into her embrace. They had been soul mates for eons of time.

Luthias eased his car into a spot by the front door. Retrieving his bagpipes and a wool blanket embellished with the tartan of the Black Clan, he hurried into the building and a waiting elevator. Exiting on the 5th floor he searched for room 504. The staff gave him a second glance, but assumed he was a messenger from the local singing telegram service. A harsh looking nurse challenged him in the hallway. Using his best English, he explained he was visiting his new granddaughter, McKenna.

"The mother and baby have been moved to room 525. Did you sign in at the nurse's station? We can't have you wandering around!"

Luthias responded, "You're a long time deid!"

Perplexed, the nurse responded, "What does that mean? I don't think I like your tone! That sounded like a threat! I'm calling security!"

In an elevated voice, Luthias retorted, "Yer bum's oot the windae!"

The nurse pushed the panic button for security. Luthias' son, Ryan had been drawn into the hallway by the familiar sounds of his father's commanding voice and a bad feeling in the pit of his stomach. The security officers arrived shortly after Ryan and the Nurse had engaged in a heated discussion. Ryan explained that his father lived more in the Scottish world and old traditions than in the current one.

The insulted nurse asked, "What did he mean by 'I'm a long time deid' and 'my bum's oot the windae'?"

Ryan smiled and explained, "It roughly translates to 'lighten up, you've got plenty of time to be a misery after you're dead' and the second one translates to 'you're talking nonsense.'"

The nurse gave Luthias a harsh look, muttering, as she walked back to her station. The security guards just snickered as they headed down the hall to make their rounds.

One of the guards mimicked a character on a popular TV show, "Nothing to see here folks, move along!"

"Dad, I'm glad you came, but do you ALWAYS have to cause an uproar when you show up?"

His father retorted, "Am no! You're always a wee scunner!"

Both men paused as they heard Ryan's wife, Ceara snicker. Ceara Taggart Black was from a Scottish and Irish background.

Her fair, ivory skin and emerald eyes were framed by her soft auburn hair. She was a tall, intelligent woman that had a fiery temper when provoked. She usually softened the blows between father and son. When that failed, she filled the role of referee between the two. Right now Ceara was trying to display a stern, disappointed face, but Luthias' comments always amused her. He had just called his son a "little whiner".

Luthias smiled at Ceara, "You're looking a bit peely-wally, but your pretty face suits the dish-cloot!"

Ryan laughed, "Trying to get out of trouble with flattery as usual."

Luthias really liked Ceara and defended, "Yer aff yer heid! She's a bonnie lass!"

Ceara smiled at the compliments, "Please you two, I'm very tired and I don't want to babysit the three of you. Let's get out of the hall so we don't disturb the others."

The trio entered the softly lit room. Luthias quietly moved to the crib in the corner. He looked down at his lovely granddaughter. She was sleeping. McKenna had her mother's fair skin, but she had strawberry blond hair. Luthias was speechless. He could hear his wife's voice as she stood next to him also admiring their new granddaughter.

Keeley touched his soul and whispered, "Guid gear comes in sma' bulk."

Luthias acknowledge, "Aye."

"I'm sorry, did you say something dad?"

"Your mother was just telling me good things come in small packages."

Ryan and Ceara exchanged concerned looks. Since the death of his wife, Luthias appeared to be in another "world." They felt he hadn't worked through his grief and let go. They had suggested several times that he should seek out counseling, but he refused. He insisted the veil between the worlds was thin and that he could travel between the worlds, visiting with his deceased wife. He also claimed his wife would visit with him. His son was also concerned his father was spending too much time alone. Luthias assured him he was surrounded by friends and that his passion, the Highland Games, along with the Celtic Heritage Centers kept him busy.

Luthias looked at the couple, "Anno what yer two thinkin, I'm radge – a mad rocket! The auld ways no longer apply. Leave me aloyn and let me enjoy the litl' wain!"

Ceara motioned to her husband to leave the room. They walked down the hall to the cafeteria.

Concerned, Ryan asked, "Do you think it's safe to leave him alone with our daughter?"

Ceara smiled and placed her hand on his shoulder, drawing him close, "I don't know, but if something happens, we're already at the hospital."

They both smiled. The past three days had been very hectic with the birth of their daughter, McKenna. Mother and child would be going home in the morning. They'd be greeted by a large reception of relatives and friends. It made Ceara even more tired thinking about it. The couple spent a few minutes in the silence of their thoughts about the future. Would they have two children to take care of, McKenna and Luthias?

Their silent moment was interrupted by the head nurse rushing down the hall calling for security and the sound of Luthias' bagpipes. The couple raced back to the room ahead of security. Ryan was furious and almost hit the nurse with the door as he rushed into the room. The matronly nurse Luthias had a previous encounter with glared at him, shaking with anger. Luthias just ignored her. The only thing that mattered was his audience, his granddaughter. Ceara could predict how this scene would end, but she was distracted by the smile of her daughter as grandfather softly played old tunes on his pipes. Security entered the room behind Ceara, but she held up her hands, motioning for them to wait a minute. They didn't see any threat, so they stood quietly, monitoring the situation. After Luthias had finished his third lullaby, he paused and looked at his other audience.

Smiling, he commented, "She's a bonnie wee lass with a fine tast' o' music!"

The angry nurse retorted, "This is NOT a music hall, if you haven't noticed, it's a HOSPITAL!"

Luthias responded, "Haud yer wheesht! Awa' an bile yer heid!"

Furious, the nurse asked Ryan, "What did he say?"

"It doesn't matter. Dad! What are you doing?"

Angrily, Luthias replied, "Whit's it look like? Playing tunes fer me granddaughter!"

The raised voices scared McKenna, causing her to cry. Ceara moved to comfort her. She wasn't happy about the commotion, but she felt sympathy towards Luthias.

Ryan tried to restrain his irritation, "Dad, I think you need to leave. We'll see you at the house tomorrow."

The nurse agreed, "Yes Mr. Black, you need to leave."

The security officers came forward to escort Luthias out of the building.

As he was leaving, Luthias looked at his son and the nurse, "A nod's a guld as a wink tae a blind horse."

Looking directly at the nurse, "You're all mouth and trousers!"

As the security officers closed the door and escorted him down the hall they heard the nurse's muffled voice, "Did he just call me a horse? What does he mean I'm 'all mouth and trousers'?"

As the elevator doors were closing, the nurse, followed by his son, were running down the hall towards him. His son was trying to explain what his father meant as the nurse was shaking her fist and shouting at Luthias.

Luthias smiled at the security guards, "Ah didnae mean to cause a stooshie, but ah'm pure scunnurt!"

The security guards had no idea what he said and didn't care. Nobody liked the head nurse and if he had insulted and upset her, it was to their amusement. Someone had turned the tables on her. Usually, she was the one pushing people around and causing a commotion. Afterwards, she'd look to security to back her up.

As Luthias drove away, his son and the head nurse continued their heated discussions while Ceara comforted and soothed her daughter.

Mother and daughter fell asleep during the drive home. Ryan was just as exhausted. He had argued with the head nurse for most of the night. She had been very insulted by the remarks his father made and escalated her complaints to the hospital director. They had a meeting with the director who determined the head nurse was over reacting, until she filed a discrimination complaint with human resources. What was a joyous occasion was fast becoming a disaster. When Ceara heard about the situation, she marched to the nurse's station and ordered the head nurse to follow her. Ceara was pissed! They went to the director's office and Ceara demanded the human resources manager join their meeting. After enduring a half an hour of Ceara's wrath, the trio agreed to her demands. Of course she reinforced them with threats of media exposure, charges of elder abuse, and a complaint to the state agencies that regulated the hospitals.

Ceara was very fond of Luthias. He had always been kind, caring, and respectful to her. He could be difficult or awkward at times, but he had a good soul and was honorable. It seemed hard to find people of Luthias' character. The world was being polluted with the "new thought and standards (or lack of)" through all venues – society, media, religion, and education.

As Ryan pulled into their drive, he noticed it was illuminated with candles. The entire house glowed from the hundreds of candles burned in honor of the new addition to his family, McKenna. A large table with a feast could be seen through the open door at the front of the house. Luthias was standing at the front door, beaming with pride. Once again he was in his regimental dress, a wool blanket fashioned with the tartan of the Black Clan draped over his arm.

Ceara woke when the car parked, McKenna stirred and yawned. Her little eyes opened momentarily and then closed again as her mother pulled the blanket around her. Ryan opened the door and helped mom and daughter out. Friends and relatives rushed over to peek at the newborn. Ryan handed various items to the group and asked them to carry them in.

As they approached his father, Luthias held the open blanket out to Ceara, "It's a sair ficht for half a loaf, but lang may yer lum reek!"

Ceara smiled and wrapped McKenna in the tartan blanket, "Thank you."

Ryan chuckled, "You don't understand what he said, do you?"

She replied, "I don't understand half of what he says, but your father has always been kind and respectful to me. I'm sure it was something nice."

Ceara smiled at Luthias again and entered her home. She just wanted to eat, a hot bath, and to sleep for a month.

Following her, Ryan translated, "It means 'Life is hard work and you only get half of what you want' and 'I wish you well for the future'."

The homecoming went well, although Ceara didn't get to sleep for a month. Luthias sent the new parents up to bed and cared for his granddaughter during the night.

As they headed to their room, Luthias told them, "Ah dinnae want you two coming doon b'for the back of eight in the morning. The wee lass and I weel be awrite."

Ceara smiled at Ryan, he explained, "Dad said he'd take care of McKenna and that he didn't want us to come down until after eight in the morning."

She responded, "Thank you. I may not get up before noon I'm so tired."

Luthias encouraged, "Aff wi you two!"

Luthias' wife, Keeley joined him as he passed the night with his granddaughter. She was the future of the Black Clan. Even though their son, Ryan had shown some interest in continuing the traditions of the Blacks, he lost interest and pursued the call of the modern world. Ryan felt traditions were fine, but they had to evolve and integrate into the new world. Just before Keeley died, she told Luthias about a dream of a granddaughter that would carry the traditions of the Black Clan. Her name was McKenna. Luthias was glad, but uncomfortable. The traditions of the Blacks had always been carried through a male lineage. Keeley assured him that McKenna would make him proud and bring honor to the Black Clan.

Luthias spent the next two weeks with McKenna and her family. After several long discussions with his son and Ceara, Luthias decided he would move to North Idaho and spend more time with his new granddaughter. Ryan and Ceara encouraged the idea so they could monitor Luthias. There was concern he might be having mental issues related to his age and the death of his wife. Luthias had a clear mind and understood what they were thinking, but didn't care, he just wanted to be with McKenna. The next day he located a rental home nearby and signed a lease. Assuring his son he would return in a couple of months after wrapping up his business and other interests, he left for Texas.

Luthias had underestimated the amount of time he'd need to conclude his business and personal matters. His greatest challenge was sorting through and packing up decades of life his home held. Everything had memories. Many nights he would sit in the candlelight visiting with these memories. Some days very little was accomplished because a smell, picture, clipping, or other item would flood him with memories. His son was concerned and offered to help him pack.

"Thenk ye, but ah can pack ma house. I'll flit in a couple of weeks."

With a concerned look, Ryan hung up the phone. Ceara was also concerned.

"What did he say?"

"He could pack his own house and he'd move in a couple of weeks."

"It's already been three months longer than we planned. I think we should go and help him move."

"What, just show up? He'd be really upset. Let's give him a little more time. Perhaps he's finally working through his grief and will be able to move on."

Ceara wasn't convinced, but she couldn't prevail against father and son once they made up their minds. Besides, she was very busy with the demands of caring for McKenna. The months advanced with Luthias not appearing to being any closer to moving. Concerned, Ceara called Luthias. He assured her he would be there before McKenna's first birthday. Finally, just two weeks before the big day, Luthias moved into his new home. He'd missed his granddaughter and was surprised at how much she had grown. She was happy to see her grandfather. Luthias would spend hours each day with McKenna. He would invite her to his house for lunch. Mom appreciated the break, but worried about them.

"Ah kin take care of the both of us. Ah hiv lots moor dangerous duties piping."

Luthias always surrounded his granddaughter with stories, music, language, and history of her Scottish heritage. He also told stories of the old ways of Ireland, before the British invasion. Much of her day was spent with her grandfather. One day, just before her fifth birthday, McKenna brought home two gifts from her grandfather.

Beaming with pride, Luthias declared, "The big box we ned to open."

Ceara objected, "You're going to spoil her. You know we don't open presents early."

That's when Ceara and Ryan heard a noise from the box.

"That sounded like a kitten."

Luthias just smiled and nodded.

Excited, McKenna shouted, "Oh! I've always wanted a kitten!"

Ryan objected, "Dad, you should have discussed this with us, FIRST."

"Guid gear comes in sma' bulk."

McKenna couldn't wait. While the adults were discussing the matter, she opened the box and out rushed a little kitten. The scared kitten crouched low to the floor and gave a weak cry.

McKenna held her arms out and called the kitten. The adults halted their discussion as they watched the little kitten rush into McKenna's open arms and purr as it licked her hand.

Luthias pronounced, "Whit's fur ye'll no go past ye!"

Ceara questioned, "What?"

Ryan explained, "It means, 'whatever is meant to happen, will happen.'"

His wife challenged, "Even if he helps it happen?"

Luthias defended, "Keep yer heid. The wee one and McKenna are awrite."

Ryan chastised, "That's not the point dad. Of course McKenna wants a kitten, but who will end up taking care of it?

McKenna spouted, "I will! I'm almost five and all grown up!"

Luthias just smiled, McKenna's parents tried to act displeased, but their daughter with a cute kitten overruled their objections.

Ryan conceded, "Okay, but you MUST promise you'll take care of…"

Luthias hinted, "MacGregor."

McKenna's parents gave him a questioning look.

"He was aboot the best china ah had."

Both of her parents didn't understand what he said.

McKenna translated, "Friend. His best friend. Grandfather told me about MacGregor. They grew up together and were pipers in the big war. MacGregor was killed early in the war."

While the others were distracted with the kitten, Ryan searched for information on his smart phone. Something wasn't right. He had one of those feelings that his father manage to produce, like the night he caused the big commotion at the hospital. Finally he found what he was looking for and held up the picture for all to see.

"I thought that little guy looked different. That's a Scottish wildcat. They're rare, endangered, and almost extinct.

"Aye."

Ceara questioned, "How did you get one?"

"Gamekeeper ah know. He had to kill it or send it to me."

"It's a wild animal! We can't let McKenna keep it!"

McKenna shouted, "MacGregor is mine! You can't take him!"

Before her parents could say any more, McKenna ran crying to her room with MacGregor. The loud slam of the door announced her intentions to defend MacGregor to the end.

Luthias proclaimed, "Ah didn't mean to cause a stooshie!"

Turning, he left for his house. At the end of the walk he looked up at McKenna's window. She and MacGregor were waving goodbye as she mouthed "Thank You". Luthias smiled, the Black Clan spirit was alive in that one.

Ryan and Ceara spent the rest of the afternoon talking with friends, a couple of veterinarians, and McKenna.

"We all agree that MacGregor can stay as long as he can behave himself as a member of our family."

McKenna nodded her head as she helped MacGregor nod in the affirmative. They were cute together.

"Okay you two, off to bed. Tomorrow is a big day! It's your birthday!"

McKenna cheered, "Yeah!"

The next morning McKenna anxiously asked, "When is Grandfather coming over?"

"He should be here in about an hour. Did you feed MacGregor?"

"Yes. MacGregor and I are going to wait out front for him."

"Okay. Don't go past the end of the sidewalk. The cars might scare MacGregor."

"He's a brave kitten! He isn't scared of anything!"

McKenna's amused parents watched her rush out the door with MacGregor enfolded in her arms.

Ceara observed, "I don't know which is tougher, that cat or McKenna."

Ryan bragged, "She gets it from my side of the family."

Ceara challenged, "All your eggs are double yoked!"

"You've been listening to my father."

"Actually, I've been listening to McKenna who has been spending a lot of time with your father. Those two are in a world of their own. I've known him a lot longer than she has and I don't understand half of what he says. McKenna can carry on a conversation in his own language for hours."

McKenna and MacGregor waited out front for over an hour.

She asked MacGregor, "Grandfather didn't forget my birthday did he?"

MacGregor just looked at her with sleepy eyes and licked his paws. A short time later her father came out and sat beside her.

"Angel, I have something to tell you. Your grandfather is in the hospital. He was in a lot of pain and the paramedics took him there early this morning. We just found out because they didn't know who to call. We're leaving in a few minutes to visit with him. You'll need to make sure MacGregor has eaten, uses the litter box, and has water in his kennel. Grandfather wanted you to bring your other present and open it at the hospital."

"Is he going to die?"

"I don't know. Let's get ready and go see him."

McKenna numbly prepared MacGregor for their absence. She worried that she wouldn't get to visit with her grandfather any more. Quietly she found her unopened present and waited by the door. The family left the house in a solemn procession.

Luthias demanded, "At lest if ye hav to keep the lines in, cover'em up! Don't want tu luk like a munster to me lil lass!"

The young nurse tried to sooth Luthias, "Now Mr. Black, please calm down. We don't know exactly what's wrong with you, but getting worked up can't help. I'll fix everything so your granddaughter won't see a thing. We deal with this all the time."

Luthias seem to calm a bit with the nurse's encouragement.

"Thenk ye."

McKenna, holding her present, raced into the room. Her parents quickly followed.

"Grandfather! Are ye awrite? Does it hurt?"

"Happy Birthday lil one! Am no hurting, but docs duno what's wrong."

"Can you come home with us and have birthday cake?"

"Soon, soon. The doc may let me leav in the morn. Open yur present."

McKenna looked at her parents who nodded their approval. Tearing away the wrapping, she opened the box.

"It's a practice chanter!"

Her mother questioned, "A what?"

Her father just groaned.

Luthias beamed, "Now ye huv yur own to practice with. As soon as ah'm weel I'll teach ye to play the practice goose."

McKenna squealed with delight, her father just groaned again.

Her mother remarked, "Somehow I don't think I'm going to like this."

Ryan explained the practice chanter was used for beginning pipers to master the mouth piece and fingerings. The practice goose was a single chanter, with a droneless bag used to transition between the practice chanter and a full set of pipes.

"And where is all this practicing going to take place?"

McKenna chimed in, "At our house and grandfather's too!"

Ceara rolled her eyes and groaned. She remembered her bothers learning to play the saxophone and flute. The first year it drove their dogs and cats crazy. The dogs would yelp and howl and the cats would hiss and run off with puffy tails. Even with their doors closed the sound traveled through the house. Ceara spent a lot of time at her friend's house and the library.

Ryan could read her thoughts, sarcastically he add, "Don't worry, it won't be that bad. In WWII the Germans called the pipers, 'the screaming ladies from hell'."

Ceara complained, "Oh great!"

Luthias pointed out, "It's gaein be awricht ance the pain has gane awa."

McKenna's mother questioned, "What?"

Her daughter translated, "It means as soon as the pesky bad stuff is out of the way, everything will be fine."

"Great."

McKenna was eager to start practicing on her new chanter. Noisily, she gave an impromptu performance of the things her grandfather had taught her. During the performance the doctor spoke with Ryan. The only thing they could determine wrong was the stress of his recent move and a vitamin deficiency. The doctor would send his father home with a month's supply of vitamins and a prescription. He assured Ryan, other than these two issues, his father appeared to be in perfect health.

Luthias was feeling much better the next morning and was released from the hospital. McKenna and her family picked him up and took him home.

"Now grandfather, you must not overexert yourself for a while and make SURE you take your vitamins. McGregor and I will watch over you until you're better. I'll play music for you and tell you stories."

Her grandfather smiled, "Guid gear comes in sma' bulk."

Ceara clarified, "McKenna insisted she took care of you, with MacGregor's help of course. We'll check in on you three through the day and bring meals over."

McKenna insisted, "Mom! I'm old enough to cook."

"Yes you are dear, but I'd like to help, if it's okay with your grandfather."

"It'll be awrite by me."

The next few months McKenna and her grandfather spent a lot of time together. McGregor grew into a rambunctious young cat.

One day, a special courier delivered a large parcel to Luthias. McKenna was anxious to open it.

"Let's wait a few minutes until your mother gets here with lunch."

"Oh please, let's open it NOW!"

"Only if you calm down, we need quiet to open the box. For now, put McGregor in the other room."

McKenna didn't like being separated from McGregor, but she knew her grandfather had a good reason for the request. When she returned, he was peering into the box and smiling. McKenna looked into the box and saw the resting animal.

"Oh grandfather, it's beautiful!"

"My friend from the Shetland Islands died last week. This little fellow has been inconsolable so they sent him to me. I thought you could help him just like you helped me."

"What's his name?"

"Copper."

"Why is he asleep?"

"He had a long ride so the vet gave him something to sleep. He should be awake in a short while and will be thirsty. Take down the new feeding bowls and fill one with water and the other with a little food."

"Okay."

McKenna's mother arrived with lunch. She knew something was different. It's something mothers know. She looked at McKenna for the answers, but McKenna didn't reveal anything.

"Okay, what's going on?"

"Nothing. Just getting some food and water down."

Her mother pointed to MacGregor's bowls, "Why does MacGregor need another set of bowls?"

The answer came to her mind. She quickly located Luthias and found him smiling as he stared into a box.

Ceara questioned, "What's going on?"

Her answer was in the box. Luthias just smiled at her.

McKenna raced into the room, "Mom don't be mad. Grandfather's friend in the Shetland Islands died last week and Copper has been very sad. He's here to visit with us while we help him get better."

"Who's Copper?"

"The dog."

"We don't need another animal. You have MacGregor. What does he think of this? Where is MacGregor?"

"He's in another room for now. This is grandfather's dog. He says it's another part of our Scottish heritage. The Shetland sheep dog was created as a compact herding dog for Shetland sheep. The standard collie was too big. The Shetland Islands are open and exposed to harsh weather. Everything is built low and compact, even the horses."

"I hope that's not of the list of cultural items to bring home."

"Grandfather and I are going to help Copper get over his grief."

Ceara looked at her daughter with skepticism.

McKenna defended, "It's true. Animals have feelings, experience fear and joy, and form friendships with others. They even have souls!"

Luthias just smiled.

Ceara looked at Luthias with hesitation, "I appreciate all that you've done for McKenna, but I'm not sure you should teach her things that might conflict with Christian values. Eventually she will have to choose her own path, but I think her parents should be the ones to help her with that."

After a moment, Luthias replied, "Am sairy ye feel that way. You're the wee hen that never layed away, but ye family clung to the ol ways while puttin on the Christian face. If the lass is to choose wisely, she needs ta know ALL the facts."

Ceara wasn't sure of everything he said, but she understood the general meaning.

"We'll continue this discussion later, in private. Your lunch is in the kitchen, I'm sure you two can manage. I have to run."

After she left, McKenna noted, "Mom isn't happy, is she?"

Luthias smiled at his granddaughter, "When people have internal conflict, it's hard for them to be satisfied with their position on a subject. Don't worry, your mom is a fine person and will do the right thing. She just needs to think about things for a while."

The pair turned their attention back to Copper.

Luthias suggested, "I think we should eat lunch and check on the little fellow later. Maybe he'll be awake when we're done."

Just as they finished lunch, McKenna and her grandfather heard a commotion in the living room. Rushing into the room, they found Copper standing beside his box, shaking. As they approached, Copper ran into the box and hid.

Luthias instructed, "Get the food and water bowls."

McKenna raced off. When she returned, he motioned for her to place them half way between the box and where they were kneeling. Slowly, Copper peered out the box. He could smell the water and the food. He was hungry and thirsty. Cautiously, the Sheltie approached the bowls. After a long drink he devoured the bowl of food. McKenna and her grandfather watched in delight. McKenna eased over to gather the bowls for a refill, but Copper scampered back into the box and growled. Her grandfather motioned for her to take the bowls and refill them. When she returned, Copper was peeking out of the box. As she placed the bowls on the floor, Copper started barking at her. MacGregor didn't like the sound of the barking and started yowling, hissing, and growling. This only excited Copper who started racing around the house looking for MacGregor. Copper ran across the floor, the couch cushions, into the open rooms and back out. Every so often he would spin in circles. McKenna and her grandfather were amused at the contest of objections and challenges between MacGregor and Copper.

Her grandfather commented, "It's a good thing you put MacGregor in another room and closed the door."

McKenna smiled as she held out a piece of food for Copper. Copper stopped and savored the aroma, but he wasn't sure about the person offering it. He advanced slowly, watching McKenna for any threatening moves. She just smiled and quietly waited for him. When Copper was only a few feet away, he paused. In a flash, he raced forward and snatched the food from her hand, quickly retreating to the safety of his box.

Over the next few days McKenna and her grandfather gained the trust of Copper and replaced his box with a bed. MacGregor was still displeased with the appearance of the dog, but he tried to ignore him. Copper had other ideas, he wanted to herd the cat. It was a test of wills. Over time the two learned to tolerate each other. Copper had his space and MacGregor his.

Between the attention McKenna provided and the companionship of Copper, Luthias regained his health. As promised, he taught her how to play the practice goose.

On a fine spring day, Luthias announced, "We're going for special treat today."

"What is it?"

"I want you to see how a band of pipers perform. We're going to see the Albeni Falls Pipes and Drums."

They spent the day at the North Idaho Highland games. In addition to the Albeni Falls Pipes and Drums, other pipe bands from the Northwest also performed at the games. McKenna was excited about the events. She was encouraged to see others striving to embrace their heritage and was determined to become the best piper in the Northwest. While she was at the games, McKenna participated in a dance class. Luthias and Keeley watched with pride as their granddaughter quickly caught on.

On the way home her grandfather commented, "Your grandmother and I are so proud of you. Soon you'll be old enough to have a full set of pipes. Your Gaelic is advancing very well. I'm also impressed at how such a young mind can remember so many of the stories and history of our people."

"That's because I can see them in my mind. I feel like I've lived some of the stories, like I've done all these things before in another life."

Luthias laughed, "Perhaps you have my little lass. Perhaps you have."

Ceara voiced her concern to her husband, "I appreciate all your father has done for McKenna, but I'm concerned. She'll be six in a few months, but she spends so much time with him and hardly any with other children. If you hadn't noticed, she is fluent in Gaelic, plays the practice chanter and goose like she's done it for a lifetime, knows more about Scottish and Irish history than Wikipedia, and can recite hundreds of Scottish and Irish tales and legends. You'd almost think she was training to be a Druid."

Ryan chuckled, "I've noticed that, but I don't see the harm. My father started me down that road, I chose a different path. He won't force her into anything, but he will encourage her."

Ceara defended, "When I visit, I sit and listen those two carry on an entire conversation in Gaelic. It's like they're in their own world. When I ask a question, they remember I'm not fluent in Gaelic and they speak English sprinkled with Scottish vernacular. I can barely understand what they're saying. Those two understand each other perfectly well."

Ryan probed, "I don't think the language, history, and stories are the real issue. You're from a Scottish and Irish background. What's really bothering you?"

Hesitating, she confessed, "The other day I stopped at your father's house to pickup McKenna. They didn't hear me come in. They were talking to someone, not each other, someone else. As I listened, I couldn't hear a third person, but they were talking to someone else. I made some noise and entered the room. They looked like they had a shared secret and pretended to be practicing Gaelic. I asked who they were talking to. Both had a guilty look as they claimed they were just practicing Gaelic. I didn't press the issue and left with McKenna."

Ryan acknowledged with a thoughtful nod, "Do you think my father is having mental issues and may hurt McKenna."

"More like he may not be in touch with reality and is influencing McKenna."

"What do you suggest?"

"I think he should have a physical and mental evaluation."

"Just how do we do that? Oh dad, we think you're losing it and are a danger to McKenna. To prove you're not, you need to get a 'clean bill of health' from a medical doctor and a shrink!"

Ceara retorted, "Of course he'll be offended if we make a demand like that. I was thinking we could encourage him to get a checkup to ensure his medication was working and there weren't any other problems."

"That might work, but what about the shrink?"

"Perhaps the doctor could perform or recommend a mental checkup to detect any possible signs or issues associated with aging."

Ryan conceded, "That might work too."

After a pause, he asked, "Who do you think they were talking too?"

Reluctantly, Ceara admitted, "My Gaelic is weak, but it sounded like they were talking to your mother."

"My dead mother?"

Ceara just numbly nodded. Ryan shook his head and called Luthias' doctor. Ryan voiced his concerns to his father about his health. He also placed the stipulation that they could no longer allow McKenna to be with him unsupervised until the issue had been resolved. If something were to happen, they felt McKenna was too young to handle the situation.

Furious, Luthias replied, "Anno what yer two thinkin, I'm radge – a mad rocket! Ah weel only do this fur the lil lass. It's a sair fecht, ye handing me a Turkish delight!"

"Please father, we're concerned about the both of you. If nothing else, do this for McKenna and our piece of mind."

"Ye think jus because am gettin auld am losin ma heid!"

Ryan defended, "We're concerned that still, after all this time, you carry on conversations with mom. Now, you're including McKenna in your conversations. She's young and easily influenced by those she adores. You're the greatest influence in her life right now, more so than her parents. It's not a bad thing, you are a great influence in Ceara's and my life, but we just have to be sure."

"Just cause ye ignore the auld ways doesn't mean they areno true. Ah weel only do this fur the lil lass. Now aff wi you and lae me aloyn to think!"

Keeley and Copper spent the rest of the night comforting him. The next day he passed his physical exam with no problems detected. The mental exam was more difficult. Luthias was insulted he had to submit to such treatment to prove he wasn't crazy. The doctor was a young, arrogant ass that assumed Luthias had mental issues. He spent the entire afternoon trying to prove he was crazy or at least starting to lose it. He found that Luthias' mind was sharper than his. He was more educated than he had expected too. During the final phase, the doctor brought Ryan and Ceara in for a conference.

Motioning towards Luthias, he explained, "On the surface, Mr. Black appears to be in perfect mental health, but I'm concerned with the hostility he exhibits. He's easily provoked and may need medication, along with anger management classes."

Luthias jumped from his chair and reached for the doctor, "I'm going ta skelp yer bahookie ye blethering glaekit eejit!"

His son intervened, "Dad please calm down and sit down."

Luthias calmed himself and returned to his seat.

The shaken doctor continued, "As you can see, he's very sensitive about dealing with his potential problems."

Ryan interrupted, "You have to understand my father, he's insulted at the idea someone imagines or accuses him of something he believes isn't true."

The doctor pointed out, "That's called denial. The very act says there's something wrong. In my estimation, it isn't safe to allow Mr. Black to be alone. He should be in a supervised environment. Here are some brochures of very nice assisted living homes."

Ceara interrupted, "The agreement was to JUST evaluate Luthias and determine IF he had any health or mental issues that might be of concern. If you and your kind had their way, EVERY child would be on medication, mindless zombies and ALL the elderly would be sedated vegetables in a nursing home. At least the ones you're not killing for their body parts. I THINK you've answered our basic questions and we'll be LEAVING now. I suggest you forget about Mr. Black and don't make me come back with a lawyer to shut your practice down."

Ceara and Luthias rose and left. Ryan just smiled at the doctor and left too.

As they were returning home, Luthias remarked, "Thenk ye. Ah hope McKenna wul visit soon."

Ceara smiled, "She'll start visiting tomorrow."

After a pause, Ceara questioned, "Who were you two talking to the other day? I know you two were talking to someone and it wasn't just Gaelic lessons."

After a few thoughtful moments, Luthias confirmed, "My wife, Keeley."

Ceara and Ryan just looked at each other. Nothing more was said for the rest of the journey. Luthias had a quiet dinner with Copper as they sat by the fire. Keeley joined the pair and passed the night with them.

McKenna came over early the next morning. Her grandfather had missed her company.

"Did the doctors say you're okay?"

"Of course they did. Most of the docs don't look like they're old enough to be out of high school. Must mean I'm getting old when they look so young. Funny how they spend all that time in school to learn knowledge our people already possessed for hundreds of years. Of course, since we don't have a piece of paper declaring our accomplishments, our knowledge is minimized."

After a moment of thought, Luthias announced, "It's time to add some depth to your knowledge of plants. We'll also introduce you to the magickal ways of our people. Your grandmother wanted you to learn another instrument from your heritage, the harp. When the clans were smaller they were called together by the clan chief with the harp or flute. As they grew, the sound couldn't carry as far. The pipes took their place not only to call the clan together, but to lead them into battle. Some called them war pipes. The English used this name as an excuse to ban them as a weapon. They were also banned from wearing the clan tartans, speaking Gaelic, and having weapons. Anyone caught violating these bans was publicly whipped and then sold into slavery or killed."

Luthias paused, "The real goal was to destroy the history and identity of our people. The English substituted their religion in place of our beliefs and the old ways. They attempted to brainwash us into not thinking of ourselves as Scottish, but part of a larger group, the United Kingdom. Most of us realized there was nothing very united about it and we refused to become part of the herd. Many of our ancestors paid with their lives, loss of their families, lands, language, and culture. Many practiced the old ways in secret. Sadly, others submitted, losing their dignity and heritage."

He continued, "The Irish had it just as bad, especially the Catholics. If they weren't killed, they were shipped as slaves to the Americas. Three hundred years before the first black slaves came to the Americas, Britain had white Irish and Scottish slaves working their plantations. They were slaves for life as were all of their descendants. When the British needed more slaves, they just rounded them up from Ireland, Wales, and Scotland. When the Americas declared their independence and won the war, Britain sent the slaves to other parts of the Empire like Australia and South Africa."

Her grandfather concluded, "It alarms your grandmother and I to see the same type of behavior, especially in the Americas.

Those in control of the government want to dictate 'correct thought', accept and encourage the mixing of races to allow us to become one, only celebrate a select few heritages while declaring 'all lives matter', rewriting history to justify their viewpoints and actions, and trying to induce shame and guilt on targeted groups to bring them into submission."

Solemnly, he looked at McKenna, "This is why it is SO important that you become the Black Clan bearer of our talents, knowledge, and gifts. We're entrusting to you these important gifts. Gifts you are to pass to the next generation. Only when people understand their history, heritage, culture, and ancestors can they move forward into the future. This will not be the only life you live on this world. You'll genetically pass these things through your blood line to your descendants and yourself. That is why it's important to not pollute your line with race mixing. Doing so dilutes your blood line and causes hardships on all. Remember, your ancestors pass two things to you, your name and your blood line. Both contain all that has been and will be."

Her grandfather requested, "Follow me, I have something to show you."

MacGregor and Copper followed the pair into an adjoining room. Standing in the corner, bathed with sunlight, was a beautiful harp. Next to the harp was a small version of the Great Highland pipes. Her grandfather smiled as her grandmother joined them.

"Your grandmother will teach you to play the harp. It was her favorite. She will also teach you how to prepare and use the plants you have studied. I will teach you about the Runes and other magick. Your grandmother will teach you how to read the flight of birds and other animals as well as other magickal subjects."

"What are these smaller pipes?"

"We call them parlor pipes. They're a smaller version of the Great Highland pipes that are played indoors. You've advanced way beyond the practice chanter and goose, but you're not large enough to handle a full size set of pipes. I had a friend ship these from Scotland. I was going to give them to you for your next birthday, but after all that has happened I think we need to start right away."

"Let's start right now!"

The trio spent the rest of the morning and that afternoon playing the harp and pipes. McKenna's mother stopped by late in the afternoon to pick her up. As she entered the kitchen, the gentle, melodic sound of harp music touched her soul. She stood there absorbing the vibrations as they soothed her soul and pealed away her barriers. They had been constructed by others and herself to keep her from having to look inward at her soul. They provided a shell of imagined comfort and reference. As she walked towards the room the harp music emanated from, she felt years of resistance melt away. She saw three people in the room, McKenna playing the harp, her grandfather smiling as he watched her play, and his wife Keeley attentively hovering around her student.

She heard Keeley gently whisper, "Pick up the tempo and intensity in the next part. Feel and play with your soul."

Smiling, Luthias walked over to Ceara, "I knew it would only take a little time until you removed the barriers."

"But she's dead!"

"Yes, in body that's true. Just because your body is dead doesn't mean your soul dies. Death is just a portal to the Otherworld to prepare for our next iteration."

"Why can't we see the dead?"

"Because we don't look."

Ceara gave him a confused look.

Luthias explained, "Many are not taught about the old ways or they've been told the old ways are evil and sinful. People go through their life building a shell of comfort and reference so they don't have to think about the old ways or why they're here. The shell is built from many things like alcohol and drugs, money and power, denial and procrastination, hobbies and sports, or work. If they keep themselves busy enough, they don't have the time to sit and quietly feel the energies of the dimensional universe and hear its whisperings. For many, the only quiet time they have is when they sleep."

She asked, "Why can I understand you so plainly? Usually, I have a hard time following much of what you say."

"Because I'm not speaking with my mouth, I'm speaking with my mind and our vibrational energies are in tune with each other.

If you'd work on your Gaelic, you could understand more of what comes out of my mouth."

McKenna finished playing and put the harp away. She smiled at her mother and took her hand.

"Tomorrow, I'll play some more. Do you want to come and listen?"

Ceara smiled, "I'd like that"

The four said their goodbyes and parted.

Later that evening Ryan noted, "You've been distracted most of the evening, is everything okay?"

"I'm fine. I was just thinking about how much our little girl of almost six has learned from her grandfather."

"Is everything okay?"

"Yes it is. Maybe we should spend a little more time as a family with your father and mother."

Puzzled, Ryan asked, "What is that suppose to mean?"

"I saw your mother today. Now, I better understand some of the things your father has been talking about."

"What?"

"Come with McKenna and I tomorrow and I'll show you."

Ryan skeptically agreed. After he visited his father's house the next day he understood what Ceara was saying. Now he had some things to think about.

As McKenna continued her lessons with her grandparents, she became a very accomplished harpist and won the top honors for the teenage age group for pipers. She was almost sixteen when her grandfather called her early one morning.

"I need you to come over early today. Can you come soon?"

"I'll be there in a few minutes."

McKenna woke her parents and told them she was going to grandfathers early. Partially asleep they acknowledge, telling her to call if she needed anything. Her inner voice prodded her to hurry. She had learned long ago to trust her promptings and raced to his home. MacGregor was right behind her. Her grandfather was watching out the front window and opened the door as she dashed up the steps.

"Good morning. I hate to wake you so early, but I need some help getting ready for my trip."

"Trip?"

"I'm feeling a bit peely-wally this morning. You're grandmother says it's nothing serious and it'll pass."

"Where are you going?"

"To be with your grandmother."

McKenna froze in her steps. She had always known the day would eventually come, but she wasn't ready to let go.

"I know what you're thinking, but I'm just following the natural cycle and leaving this tired old shell here. We can still visit and we'll be watching."

"But it won't be the same!"

"No it won't, but you won't be alone."

As they walked through the house her grandfather handed her an envelope.

"These are all the legal papers you'll need. I'm leaving everything to you. That includes the Black name and bloodline. Continue to bring honor to your roots. Copper isn't going and will need some comfort. Will you take him as your friend?"

Teary eyed, she replied, "Of course."

Luthias instructed, "Light some candles in the front room and play some beautiful harp music to send me on my journey."

McKenna paused as she finished lighting the candle, "Who are all these people?"

"Our ancestors. They've come to welcome me to the Otherworld. Don't be shocked, they're here all the time. They just have different vibrational energies than we do, so most people can't or don't want to see them."

McKenna sat down at the harp and called Copper to her side. MacGregor had already settled near her feet.

Her grandfather said goodbye to Copper and urged, "Now go on my friend, McKenna will look after you. I want you to look after her."

Her grandfather leaned over and kissed McKenna on the head.

"Be strong and make sure you play the pipes at my funeral. I'll see you when you get to the other side."

Her grandfather rested on the divan. Through her silent tears, McKenna played a soothing, haunting melody from her heart. She had not practiced this song, but from somewhere deep in her soul, from another life, it poured out. She watched her grandfather take his last breath and rise from his body. He smiled as he passed by and into the open arms of Keeley.

McKenna called her parents and told them of his death. The next few hours became a whirlwind of confusion with the paramedics, coroner, and police reports. By late morning calm had replaced the tumult. McKenna locked up the house and left with Copper and MacGregor.

A few days later, dressed in the Black tartan, McKenna wailed out a series of songs on the pipes that touched the souls of all in attendance at Luthias' funeral. Luthias had also been dressed in the Black tartan. Just before they closed the casket, McKenna placed her practice chanter in his hands.

"Thanks, grandfather."

Luthias and Keeley smiled at their granddaughter.

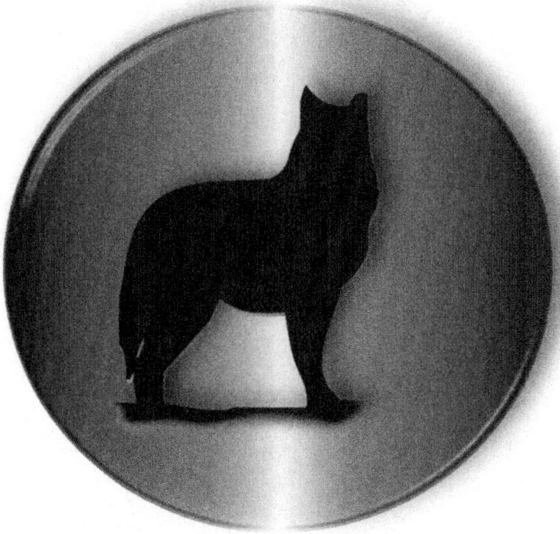

Allen Hartley

Chapter 6
Nature

For days we sailed in a violent storm. Our antagonist pursued and harassed us constantly. The Otherworld walker had warned us of the dangers that would harry our quest to the forbidden land. Our group remained strong and unshaken. All had seen the ill omens that spoke of our future, except myself. I had not reacted as the others, which caused suspicions and whisperings to race through the ranks of my fellow adventurers.

The murmuring turned into grumbling and threats. My companions became so focused on my inert reactions to the omens they ignored the creature that threatened to destroy us.

One of the adventurers pointed his finger at me and spoke the feelings of the group, "Why didn't you see the omens! Perhaps the sea creature is after you! We should offer you to him and save ourselves."

As the group drew their weapons, I stood motionless with my hands held out from my sides. Looking into their eyes, they detected a shift in my energies.

Someone shouted, "He's a monster too! Look! He's changing form!"

The adventurers fell over themselves as I shifted to a great, black wulf. I lunged forward and ripped the throats from the three closest men. In concert with the sea monster, I caused my former companions to scurry to the side of the ship where they were consumed. Mayhem usurped order as all tried to save themselves. When none were left, the sea monster acknowledged my presence and slipped below the turbulent waters. I retained my wulf form and went below to rest. The ship would travel to its destination under the influence of an Otherworld crew.

Later that night, the sea calmed and a full moon, accompanied by a host of stars greeted my visit on the deck. Large masses of ice floated by like passing ships as fingers of cold, crisp air gently caressed my fur. The energy levels were rising as we neared our destination.

In the early morning light I could see the approaching shoreline. Over the roar of the surf that clawed the rocky beach, I could hear the faint sound of rushing water. The alpine landscape rose to meet the cliff walls that formed the mountain's base. Mountains that rose so high, they seemed to scrape the clouds from the sky.

My destination was the source of the fast flowing waters that rushed out to meet the sea. Her name was Sulis, the Spring

Goddess. Sulis would provide knowledge, powers, and the energies required to find and meet with Inanna, the Goddess of Nature.

My purposes were my own. They had been secreted away from the view of others. When I found Sulis on a high rocky outcrop, she didn't ask my reason for wanting an audience with Inanna.

"I can't tell you where to find her, but I can give you the powers and knowledge to find her. What she will do with you, only Inanna knows."

I replied, "I thank you in advance for your assistance. I have traveled many life times, ascending to a level that will allow me to remain in the presence of Inanna."

"So I can see. Spend some time with me and learn. I'll enjoy the company."

Early one morning, after spending months with Sulis, I trotted off in search of Inanna. Her energy projections were elusive. They were in everything she touched. After frustrating days of searching, I rested under an oak tree at the edge of a meadow. Scanning the area I could feel Inanna's strong energies, but I couldn't locate her. Out of frustration I projected her name.

In my mind, she answered, "What is it you seek?"

I responded, "An audience with Nature's creator, Inanna."

She encouraged, "Enter the meadow and you shall find me."

As I entered the meadow, Inanna appeared. I ran over and sat in front of her, tail wagging.

"I know what you seek, but I will ask for a favor in return."

Nature is about flowing, renewal, cycles, order, efficiency, and evolving. Eight Runes compose the Bind Rune representing Nature. Just as the tree sends its roots into the soil to seek the nutrition it needs, the Bind Rune for Nature has roots at its base, drawing energies, knowledge, and power from its environment. The mid section of the Rune shows fulfillment from the resources drawn in by the roots. As the new growth of a tree progresses in stages through the year, the growth of the Nature Bind Rune reflects this same cycle. When the tree has completed a life cycle, it dies, returning its earthly shell to the land. Another generation follows, pushing skyward as they renew the cycle.

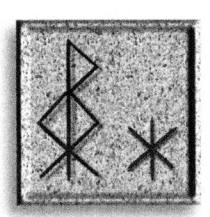

Hagalaz/Haggall ᚺ or ✳ is the Rune of completion and the number nine, a very powerful magickal number. Hagalaz/Haggall is also the Rune of destruction, disaster, and chaos. In nature, new beginnings or cycles occur after the current cycle has been disrupted or concluded through events such as death, fire, flood, storms, volcanoes, earthquakes, blizzards, or any other display of Nature's cleansing forces. It is important to cleanse, purify, and return the elements to their origin. This provides resources for the next cycle.

Only humans perceive our existence as near static and are traumatized when our concept of this world is reorganized through a natural cycle of Nature. We deceive ourselves trying to create a static environment in a natural world that is constantly evolving. The only constant in Nature is change. If we are to evolve to a higher plane of existence we have to seek out change and growth. This doesn't have to be a solo journey, but as companions we should contribute to the growth of each other. Ultimately, it is our responsibility to follow the path leading to our progression.

Berkano/Bjarkan ᛒ represents new beginnings, fertility, birth, and growth. It is the feminine Rune of nurturing and magick. It signifies cleanliness and purity. The Birch is the first tree to come into leaf after the winter season, representing renewal, rebirth, and inception. This slender, determined tree represents the seed potential of all growth and is hardier than the mighty Oak. Winter is Nature's cleansing and sabbatical season for our world. The new year/cycle begins at the winter solstice. After the winter gestation, new life emerges with spring.

Sowilo/Sól ᛋ is the Rune of the Sun. It also represents the lightning bolt, the spark of life. As new life emerges in the spring, the Sun continues to nurture it into fullness with the warmth of summer.

Laguz/Lögur ᛚ is associated with water. This element, in conjunction with the Sun, is vital to all of nature. It is also associated with edible roots such as onions, leeks, and garlic. These are used for cleansing, healing, and protection from poisons.

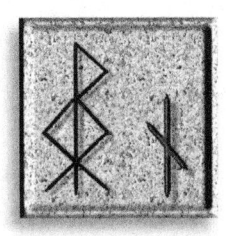

Nauthiz/Nauð ᚾ is the Rune of trials, endurance, projection of the will, and self sufficiency. "What doesn't kill you makes you stronger!" Nature uses this principle to build the strong and cull the weak or obsolete. The vanity of humanity believes they need to save everything. It is that same vanity that leads humans into the false belief that they are the "masters" of the world. This belief has been propagated through false religious teachings and is woven into the fabric of our societies. Stand before the cleansing force of the erupting volcano or the heat of the wildfire and declare the supremacy of humanity. In your last few seconds of this existence, you'll be answered by the roar of Nature as you're deleted from the gene pool. Hold your weapons high and challenge the lighting bolts of Nature. Change the path of the magnificent tornadic winds or if you can, dissipate them. What human can stand against or contain the force of the rushing waters from Nature's floods or those of the raging seas?

The same storm which destroys life also brings the nourishing rains and potential for creating anew.

Wisdom of Eosphoros

There are those that can work with Nature and influence the elements, but they aren't constrained by the shackles of organized religions. They live within the cycles of Nature and understand they are part of, not superior too, much less masters of nature.

Most of humanity is so puffed up to think they are the only one with souls. This incorrect thinking allows them to commit gross violations against Nature. They have been taught to ignore the idea that all that exists in our world has intelligence and a soul. If we would only look and listen, we could perceive the souls and intelligence of all that exists. There is much to learn from Nature. Our ancient ancestors possessed this knowledge, but centuries of deletions, revisions, and edits to our ancestral knowledge by the church or others has left many helpless and ignorant. Time spent with nature can help us reconnect with the knowledge from our ancestral pool and our past lives.

*You can easily judge the character of a man
by how he treats those who can do nothing for him.*

Johann Wolfgang von Goethe

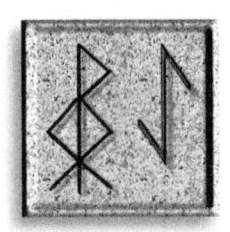

Eihwaz/Eoh ᛇ is the Rune of death and renewed life, a continuation of existence and our life journeys. The tree associated with this Rune is the Yew. The Yew is a powerful magickal and defensive ally. It is used to make bows for hunting and defense. Magickal items were also made from Yew wood. The wood or leaves of the Yew were laid upon graves of our ancestors to remind the departed spirits that death was only a pause in life before rebirth. The great world tree, Yggdrasill that connects all, is a Yew tree.

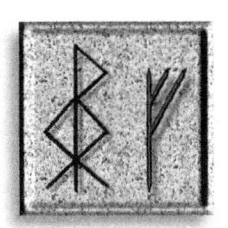

Fehu/Fé ᚠ Is the physical manifestation of the will. It represents the physical form for the soul to inhabit in this world.

*Matter is merely "interrupted energy or force,"
that is, energy or force at a low rate of vibration.*

The Kybalion

Many are lead to believe that ONLY humans have a soul and everything else responds to our world organically through stimuli. All that exists has not only a worldly shell, but a soul. If it doesn't have a soul, it is a dead shell. It is from the spark of life found in Sowilo/Sól that Fehu/Fé, the physical manifestation of the will is possible. At a higher level, Fehu/Fé represents one of the manifestations of the ALL in the comos.

Do not make the mistake of supposing that the little world you see around you—the Earth, which is a mere grain of dust in the Universe—is the Universe itself. There are millions upon millions of such worlds, and greater. And there are millions of millions of such Universes in existence within the Infinite Mind of THE ALL. And even in our own little solar system there are regions and planes of life far higher than ours, and beings compared to which we earth-bound mortals are as the slimy life-forms that dwell on the ocean's bed when compared to Man. There are beings with powers and attributes higher than Man has ever dreamed of the gods' possessing. And yet these beings were once as you, and still lower—and you will be even as they, and still higher, in time, for such is the Destiny of Man as reported by the Illumined.

The Kybalion

Jera/Ár ᛡ is the Rune of cycles – life cycles, lunar cycles, and yearly cycles. Many are incorrectly taught and believe our lives are linear and end at death. Our lives are a continual cycle of rebirth, growth, and death. Nature provides the true pattern for the cycles. Once we exit this world through the doorway of death, we prepare for our next iteration in this or another world. There are many things to learn and experience as we ascend to our higher states.

The Runes and Nature have a very close connection. For those that can still themselves, honor and observe both, they will share their secrets. Nature is a powerful force and is found all around us, no matter where we are. To see, all one has to do is look. To hear, all on has to do is listen.

Like our ancestors, we are immersed in Nature. Some welcome and invite Nature into their lives, others are fearful or repulsed by it and attempt to exterminate it.

*Nature is painting for us, day after day
pictures of infinite beauty*

John Ruskin

Raccoon's Feast

*The raccoon, waddled and toddled, to the lake
A fine feast, he would partake
Fishing and swishing his food, he became very rude
A turtle, had climbed the hurdle, of a log
To swoon the raccoon, and enjoy the feast*

Many stories and legends from our ancestors are intertwined with interactions and relationships between humans and animals. In some cases, those with advanced abilities and powers can shift between human and animal forms. In Irish, Scottish, and Faroese folklore, the Selkie or Seal People are prominent. Selkies were imbued with magickal abilities and could shift from their seal form to human form. During the transformation they shed their seal skin. If the seal skin was taken, the Selkie couldn't transform back and return to the sea. Selkie spouses were acquired by taking and hiding their seal skins. If the Selkie found their seal skin, they would transform back and return to the sea.

I wrote a short story about a human and Selkie relationship, *Summer Love* for the February 2014 issue of the Celtic Guide magazine. It is written as historical fiction like three of my published books, *Secrets of the Soul*, *Mists of Dawn*, and *Boundaries of Time*.

Summer Love

The Council of the Gods was in an uproar over the tide of the new religion spreading across the lands. It was sweeping aside the old ways in an attempt to extinguish them. Their followers were being forced to convert or die. Their legends, history, magick, and knowledge were being polluted, stolen, and corrupted. Using a program of torture, intimidation, and bribery, the weak were embracing the new religion and the strong were being trampled.

"Albion! Step forward!" Commanded the Head of the council.

"We're charging you with the task of finding a strong follower that can be entrusted with our powers, knowledge, and treasures. It is our conclusion that we're in the nigredo aspect of our existence. As with all the cycles, we will transition with this one too. We need fertile ground to winter the seeds of our ways until they can emerge in the spring of a new era."

Albion responded, "It's my honor to serve the Council of the Gods!"

The Council Head motioned to his assistant.

"We place in your trust, our two most prized items, the gold and silver adder stone and the sword, Fragarach. Bestow these upon a strong and worthy follower as well as the gifts of our magick and knowledge."

"I already have a candidate in mind," Albion assured them.

"Go with our blessings and fulfill your charge," the Head of the council admonished.

Albion returned to his undersea home and enlisted the aid of his daughter, Muireann. He had foreseen the approaching diminishment and elimination of his people under the new religion. Shortly before his meeting with the Council of the Gods, he had watched a young mother place her newborn son in a basket on the seashore. The incoming tide swept the infant into the sea. Her lover and the boy's father, was a Selkie. He had returned to the sea before the child was born. It didn't escape the notice of the new religious leaders that the mother was without a husband. Under the old ways, it was acceptable and an honor to have a Selkie child. Many times, the call of the sea was so great, the child would join the Selkie parent.

Selkies, sent by Albion guided the basket to a remote northern island. Albion named the boy Muirios. The basket came to rest on the rocky beach of the island. A fisherman and his young daughter, Keeley were its only inhabitants.

Early each morning, Keeley would stroll the rocky beach in search of useful items that had washed up during the night. The storm from the previous night had washed up large clumps of kelp and wood. As she returned for her third load, Keeley noticed the basket. She rushed to it, eager to investigate the contents. To her surprise, the smiling face of a baby boy greeted her. Excited, Keeley snatched up the basket and raced home. She placed the basket next to the tiny stove to warm the infant. After a while, she lifted him from the basket to change his damp clothes. To her surprise, the basket, blankets, and baby were warm and dry.

The babe started to fuss and squirm. Keeley guessed the infant was hungry, but she had no milk. She filled a pot of boiling water with pieces of kelp and fish. After the mixture had boiled down, she placed the pot outside to cool. Using a piece of rolled kelp as a funnel, she fed the warm meal to the infant. As she held him in her arms, the satiated child drifted off to sleep.

Later that afternoon, her father returned empty handed after a day of fishing. When Keeley presented the baby, her father was furious.

"Take the basket and baby back to where you found it! I can't feed another mouth. I can barely feed us. Since your mother died, we've had a tough go of it! Look at us! What will we eat tonight? Kelp and bark I suppose."

Keeley knew her father was right. Fighting back the tears, she placed the infant in basket and slowly made her way to the flat rocks near the water. She placed the babe on the rocks and said her goodbyes. As she turned to leave, she heard a woman's voice. Turning quickly in the direction of the voice, she saw a smiling seal bobbing in the water.

The seal spoke again, "Please take Muirios and care for him."

"You can speak!" the excited Keeley squeaked.

The seal disappeared. After a few minutes, she returned and deposited five large fish on the flat rock next to the infant.

"Take Muirios and the fish back to your father. The sea God, Albion has a plan for the young boy. Care for him and we will protect and provide for you. Return here each afternoon just before sunset and collect the fish from the rock."

Keeley asked, "How can you speak?"

"I'm a Selkie," the seal replied.

"The seal people!"

"Yes. Now take the fish and infant back home and explain to your father what we have discussed."

Keeley hurried back. The fish and baby filled her arms.

"Where did you get all those fish? Why do you still have that baby?" Her father scolded the young girl.

Keeley gave him one of her looks that softened his tone and allowed her to explain.

"You know I've always believed what you've told me, but...a Selkie? I've never seen one, but I've never seen a water dragon either," her father retorted.

Relenting, her father declared, "I'll trust you on this, but it will be your responsibility to raise the child. I will help all that I can, but you know I'm at sea most of the time."

Keeley gave her tough father a kiss on the cheek and a big hug that melted him in his seat. Afterwards, she took her new brother into her room and tucked him in bed.

Years flowed by and the boy grew to be a young man of 12. One afternoon Keeley went to the rock to collect the fish and was greeted by a new Selkie with 17 fish. The new Selkie instructed her to take the young man to the local village. In the village lived a Druid who would become Muirios' mentor.

Keeley, her father, and Muirios made the three day journey to the village and located the Druid. He agreed to take Muirios as his apprentice. After a tearful parting, Keeley and her father left the village. Not far from the village, the soldiers of the new religion detained the pair and accused them of conspiring with the Druids. The inquisitors declared them to be heretics and the soldiers executed them.

The soldiers and inquisitors entered the village, forcing everyone into the main square. Using his magick, Muirios' master made the pair invisible allowing them to escape. The villagers weren't so fortunate.

"We must travel far to the north, beyond the outer islands if we hope to complete your training. We have 17 years of work before you're prepared," his master revealed.

Muirios questioned, "Prepared for what?"

"For the rite of Aisling."

"Rite of Aisling?"

"Your rite of Enlightenment. You will spend 17 years preparing and then it is up to the Gods to decide if one or more of them will accept you as their vassal. You'll speak for them and they'll speak through you. They'll bestow knowledge, powers, and magick IF you're worthy and ready," his master answered.

Muirios questioned, "And if I'm not ready?"

"You'll either go mad or will be struck down."

Over the next 17 years, Muirios progressed steadily through his training. He did struggle with maintaining focus. Visions and fantasies of his Selkie lover flooded his mind. Finally, he completed the program to his master's satisfaction.

After the evening meal, his master revealed, "Tomorrow we journey to the Eye of the Water Dragon. There, we'll prepare you for the rite of Aisling. Alban Heruin, the Light of the Shore is the day appointed for your Enlightenment."

"Midsummer?" Muirios queried.

"Of course. As you know, it is one of the three days in the cycle that the Otherworld is the closest. Now rest. We have a long journey ahead," his master admonished.

Muirios tossed and turned all night. In the pink light of the early dawn, his master led him to the beach and a waiting boat. The small craft glided swiftly over the glassy waters. Overhead, the gulls "laughed" at the seafarers. Muirios' thoughts turned to the sea and its mysteries. Much to his master's displeasure, he had displayed an intense infatuation with the stories about Selkies. The apprentice couldn't resist. He didn't understand why he was so drawn to them. One Selkie in particular filled his dreams and fantasies. She was tall with auburn hair that fell below her waist. Her soft, pale skin heightened the color of her steel blue eyes. Her curvaceous body filled a tight, form fitting dress made from sealskin, her sealskin! Often she would speak to him in his dreams. Her voice sounded like the gentle flowing waters of an inland stream rushing out to embrace the sea.

"Your mind should be focused on more serious matters than the Seal People! ESPECIALLY that one! There is nothing but sorrow for those who embrace a Selkie lover," his master chastised.

Nothing more was said for the remainder of the journey. Each was left to his own thoughts.

As the tiny vessel maneuvered to a beach in the deep inlet, Muirios questioned, "What is this place? I feel very powerful magick here."

His master replied, "It is a place of power. The joining of the sea, sky, and land make it a powerful place between our world and the Otherworld. That power is magnified by the water dragon that lives here."

Muirios became uneasy at the mention of a water dragon. They were very dangerous and ill tempered.

Seeing his apprentice's uneasiness, his master soothed, "The water dragon I speak of was slain eons ago when the hero, Assipattle rammed the dragon with his boat and set his liver on fire. As the dragon died, his teeth fell out and made the islands to the north, near the Danes. His tongue made the sea of the Danes and we have entered his eye. His head makes the land you see before you. His left leg made the island we passed a short while ago."

His master informed him, "This place is called Eriboll."

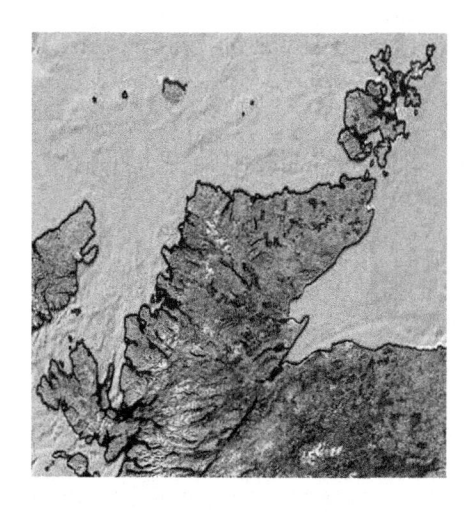

He commanded, "Come. We must prepare you for your Aisling. Gather wood and make two large piles in front of that cave. We will make wild fire to purify your body and soul. Afterwards, I will leave with the boat and you can begin your meditation. Tomorrow is Alban Heruin and will be the day of your enlightenment."

After starting the wild fires using only specially prepared sticks and bark, his master tossed herbs and prepared powders into them. Giving Muirios a warm potion, he instructed him to jump over the fires to purify his body and soul. While he was focused on jumping over the fires, his master and the sun left him.

Even though he was alone and hungry, Muirios continued to jump over the fires through the night and into the predawn of the morning. The exertion overwhelmed him. He collapsed on the soft sands of the beach. The incoming tide washed over his body waking him from his dreams. Dreams about Selkies. The purification fires were reduced to smoldering mounds and the warm morning sun climbed high into the sky as Muirios tried to meditate. His mind continued to wander amongst the images and stories of Selkies. Especially, his fantasy Selkie with long auburn hair. He could almost hear her whispers and feel her touch. Her lips pressed lightly on his. Soon their passions climaxed and they wrestled in love's embrace.

A flash of light and the crash of thunder jolted Muirios from his dreams. It was dark and the rain pounded the beach with its projectiles. Muirios sought shelter in the cave. His mind drifted back into the world of his Selkie lover. Her gentle touch caused his fires within to ignite. He raced off with her in the heat of passion.

He awoke to the silence of the new morning, realizing his failure. He had squandered his time for enlightenment with dreams of his Selkie lover. His master would be furious! 17 years of training had been wasted. He would return disgraced to face his disappointed master.

At first, his master just sank down in his chair. After a few minutes, he jumped to his feet and ordered Muirios out of his home.

"You were the last hope we had against the wave of the new religion! I can't believe you've wasted the opportunity with fantasies of Selkies! The old ways and our Gods will surely perish. Be gone with you!" His master ordered.

Reluctantly, Muirios left, walking aimlessly down the street and out of the village. For days he wandered the countryside until familiar landmarks began to appear. He was near his home and family! After visiting with the fishermen at the pier, he convinced one of them to take him to the island that was his boyhood home.

"Not many a one goes out here. A crazy witch that talks to Selkies lives there. Some say she even has a Selkie lover. Not good to be accused of these things with the inquisitors running about the countryside. I heard a boat was hired to take some of the soldiers of the new religion and inquisitors to pay her a visit. Half way across, the Selkies attacked the boat and killed everyone in it." The old fisherman continued his ramblings.

Muirios questioned, "Do the Selkies attack your boat?"

"Naw! I'm just an old fisherman who don't bother anybody. Besides, I feed the baby seals and help the injured ones."

The old boat bumped against the rocky shore and Muirios disembarked.

"Thank you again for the ride."

"No problem. It's on the way to my favorite fishing spot."

Muirios made his way to the weather battered house of rock and moss. Memories flooded his mind of his early childhood with his sister and father. He found the front door ajar. Pushing it open, he saw his beautiful sister sitting by the fire in an old rocking chair.

"Welcome home brother. I've missed you so," she greeted.

"I have missed you and our home too. Where is father?"

"Out fishing."

Muirios was uneasy when he realized the old fisherman that had given him passage to his home was his father. He hadn't recognized him!

"When will he return?"

His sister hesitated, "After we left you in the village, we were detained by the soldiers of the new religion. The inquisitors accused us of conspiring with the Druids and condemned us as heretics. We were executed by the soldiers."

Stunned, he replied, "Then the old fisherman is…"

"The Otherworld spirit of your father. He wanted to visit with you one more time when you were a man and Druid," she revealed.

"And you?"

"I was reborn again into the cycle of life. As a young woman I took a Selkie lover. He was torn between two women, the sea and myself. I chose to remain with my lover and became a Selkie, a part of the Otherworld."

Shocked, her brother sat down.

After a period of silence, he hung his head and confessed, "I didn't complete my Aisling…I was too distracted with fantasies of Selkies. I have failed in my apprenticeship as a Druid."

His sister rose and glided to him. Gently stroking his head with her hand she comforted, "Albion has a great path for you. It's in your Wyrd that you and a companion will preserve the seeds of the old ways. The new religion has corrupted, stolen, and destroyed the traditions of our ancestors and those who preserve and honor it. A great wave of darkness is washing across this land and our people. Like the snows of winter and floodwaters of early spring, this darkness will recede. The new growth of spring will emerge and blossom into summer's bounty. The new religion will wither and decay as all things do in the wheel of the year."

Allowing him to comprehend her words, she instructed, "Go to the inlet and take the boat to the Eye of the Water Dragon. Remain there and prepare yourself for the next Alban Heruin. Albion will bestow his gifts upon you. This will be your Aisling and Wyrd."

He asked, "What of yourself?"

"I return to my lover and children," she replied.

Muirios watched as she walked to the waters edge and transformed into a seal. Gracefully, she plunged into the sea and disappeared beneath the waves.

Looking at the table, Muirios noticed a large plate of fish. Ravaged with hunger, he consumed the meal. Searching through the house, he found supplies for his journey. In the pantry he found 17 smoked fish and loaves of bread.

By the soft light of a rising moon, he rowed the small boat into the calm seas. Navigating the currents, Muirios found a westward flow that would carry him to the Eye of the Water Dragon.

During the months that followed, Muirios spent his time preparing for the Alban Heruin in meditation and reflection. He furnished his cave comfortably with treasures and resources of the land and sea. As the time of midsummer approached, he made the final preparation for the cleansing fires on the beach. Using his knowledge of astronomy, he had calculated the position of the high point of the sun. A rock was positioned to cast its shadow between the fires when the sun reached its apex.

On the eve of Alban Heruin, he lit the fires and began his ritual of purification. After spending hours of jumping over the fires, Muirios collapsed on the beach to rest. Once again he drifted off into dreams about his Selkie lover.

An abrupt smack from the flat of a boat oar woke him from his dreams. Dragon boats covered the beach and the inlet. His fires had attracted the attention of a Viking raiding party.

The leader demanded, "What are you doing on our sacred ground?"

"Your ground? I didn't know it had been claimed," Muirios responded.

The second in command pulled him up and slapped him with the back of his hand.

"Our ancestors have claimed this land since the beginning of time!"

"I apologize for trespassing. I came here for my enlightenment," Muirios defended.

One of the raiders returned from his search of Muirios' boat and cave. After a hushed discussion with the leader, he nodded and sprinted off.

The leader challenged, "It appears that you have no value. We have journeyed far from our homes in search of wealth, women, and any other treasures we can find. It obvious you're not a woman and you don't have any wealth. What can you provide in exchange for your life?"

One of the raiders suggested, "What about entertainment!"

The others cheered as they drug Muirios to the stakes that had been driven into the rocks and sand. They tied him to the stakes and took turns punching and kicking him until he bled. One of the party attempted to cut him with a knife, but the firm grasp of the leader prevented it.

"If you kill him now you won't get to see him wiggle about when the sharks come to feast," the leader admonished.

Turning to Muirios, the leader informed him, "Boy! Let this be a lesson to you and any others that dare enter our sacred cove, they will meet death from the sea! It's low tide now, but that will change when the sun reaches its midpoint on the midsummer's day. Notice you're on an incline. Your shoulders and lower parts of your body should be in deep enough water for the sharks to feast on while you watch."

The raiders' laughter followed in their wake as they turned to enjoy their mead on the beach, waiting for the tide to return.

As the tide crept inward, the leader ordered some of his men to chum the water with pieces of fish and blood to attract the sharks. Some of the drunken men almost fell overboard while chumming. Muirios felt the first shark brush against his leg. It didn't bite him, but its rough, sandpaper hide peeled skin from his leg, causing it to bleed. The salt water on the wound burned him like fire. The raiders cheered. Many were betting when the first bite and limb would be taken.

Just when Muirios had given up hope, the sky began to darken with clouds and the sea became absolutely still. The seafaring raiders knew this was a bad omen. Suddenly, the boats exploded and the men were expelled into the sea. The only thing marking their watery grave was the turbulent, boiling waters that contained parts of the sharks and their companions. The raiders on the beach began to realize it was not the sharks consuming their companions, but something was consuming both of them.

As they watched, a seal emerged from the waters beside their captive. Slowly, the seal stood as it transformed into a beautiful woman. She had long, flowing auburn hair. Her covering was a sealskin garment. Releasing their captive, the Selkie escorted him to the beach. The petrified raiders watched the final stages of her transformation into human form. They had heard of the Otherworld people, the seal people, but they were supposed to be legends! With one mind, the raiders abandoned their equipment and provisions, fleeing in terror.

"You're a Selkie! The one I've seen in my dreams!" Muirios exclaimed.

"Yes. I'm the daughter of Albion, a sea God. He has sent me to you as a gift. I have other gifts to give you from Albion and myself. We have been chosen to be keepers of the knowledge, powers, and treasures of our people and the ways of the Gods. At a future time these things will spring forth just as the seeds of spring wake from their slumber."

Reading his many thoughts, she replied, "My name is Muireann."

"Mine is Muirios," he excited replied.

"Yes, I know. My father and I have watched over you for many years."

She moved closer to him and caressed his face.

"At first it was my duty to assist my father, but as I came to know you, something deeper grew. I have visited you many times in your dreams and have waited for this moment."

Muirios could feel her intoxicating energies flow through his soul.

"I feel I have known you all my life," he replied.

"Not just this life, but other lifetimes," she corrected.

Removing her sealskin clothing, she folded it and placed it at his feet. She placed the gold and silver adder stone and the sword, Fragarach inside her sealskin.

Muireann spoke, "I offer my sealskin and myself to you. As long as you possess the sealskin I won't return to the sea. Hide it from my sight, the sea calls me through it. As much as I desire to be with you, the sea's call is unstoppable. Only as a Selkie can you follow me."

As he lifted her up, he promised, "If I have to forsake my life for that of a Selkie to be with you, then so be it!"

"It is not as easy as it might seem," she warned.

As Muirios knelt to pick up the sealskin, he felt a heavy object within it. Opening the sealskin he found the sword, Fragarach and a gold and silver adder stone. He looked at her inquisitively.

"Those are gifts from the Gods. Nothing can resist the cutting of the sword, Fragarach and nothing is hidden from the gold and silver adder stone. I have other gifts and knowledge to bestow upon you from the Gods."

He wrapped the sword and adder stone in her sealskin and placed them in his sea bag.

After a pause, she offered, "Would you enter into a Teltown Marriage with me on this midsummer's day?"

"You mean for a year and a day?"

"Yes."

"And after that?"

"We'll consider that at a future time. For now, let's focus on the present," she responded.

Muirios questioned, "Who will give their consent, blessing and be our witnesses?"

Bending down, she scooped water from a pool into her hand. Dipping her hand in the water, she wiped it across his brow removing his veil and allowing him to see the Otherworld.

Sweeping her hands all around she replied, "The Gods and inhabitants of the Otherworld give their blessing, consent, and will be our witnesses."

Joined in a Teltown Marriage, the couple spent the remaining night consummating their union on the beach in the soft light of the moon and warm glow of the fire.

As they prepared to leave, Muireann announced, "I am pregnant, with twins. A boy and a girl."

Muirios stammered, "What? How can this be?"

"It is part of our Wyrd," she soothed.

She revealed, "Search your soul and find the other gifts that I have bestowed upon you."

Muirios reflected inward. He could detect strong, new energies in his soul.

"What are these energies?"

"They're the knowledge and powers of the Gods and our collective ancestors that will be passed to future generations. You can unlock them through your meditations and journeys to the Otherworld. I will be your guide."

After a pause, Muirios proclaimed, "I need to visit my old master and share all these wonderful things with him."

Muireann warned, "It is not safe to journey to that part of the country. You'll find nothing but heartache there."

He replied, "That may be true, but I still need to visit with him and make things right. We didn't part on good terms. He devoted 17 years of his life to prepare me for my Aisling and I failed him the first time. I have succeeded the second time."

She warned again, "Many in the old ways have succumbed to the new religion by force and bribery. Our traditions have been polluted and corrupted. Even though your master is strong, he may have been turned too."

"I REFUSE to believe that! He was devoted to preserving our Gods and the old ways of the people," Muirios defended.

After a moment of silence, she conceded, "It will be as you say. We will go and visit with your old master. Let's spend the night at your old home. I visited you many times in my other form. I wanted so many times to transform and feel your embrace, but it was forbidden. Would you grant me this request before we visit your old master?"

Walking over to her, he took her hands and gazed into her eyes.

"I've always had dreams about you…now you are here and I'm powerless to deny your request."

Sweeping her up, she giggled as he carried her to the boat. As he lowered into the boat, she pulled him on top. Their journey was delayed for another two hours.

They arrived at his old home in the early evening. After securing the boat and gathering their bags, the couple proceeded down the shore to the rock and moss house. Faint candlelight seeped through the cracks in the door and the opaque windows.

Muireann observed, "There must be someone inside!"

"I don't know who it would be. My sister, Keeley returned to the sea and her Selkie lover."

Cautiously, the couple opened the door and ventured inside. Flowers decorated the room as the warm firelight washed over it. The table was covered with a fine cloth and illuminated by golden candles. A feast with drink waited for them on the table. Muireann peered into the bedroom and tugged on Muirios' arm.

"Someone must have been expecting us!"

Muirios was puzzled, "Yes, but who knew we were coming?"

The bed had been made with clean, satin sheets. A large velvet comforter rested on top of the sheets. Four large pillows were at the top of the bed. Rosemary, Lilac, and Lavender had been spread around the room. Their fragrance mingled with the incense and candles.

Muirios opened the envelope lying on top of the comforter.

"Dearest Brother and Sister,

We wish you well in your path together. Enjoy this night, it is your night.

Your loving Sister"

Muirios spoke first, "Shall we eat first?"

Muireann pushed him down on the bed.

Later that evening, the couple sat next to each other as they shared their meal.

Muireann teased, "I think we were suppose to sit across from each other."

He replied, "I like this better. For decades I've had dreams about you. Even when it displeased my Druid master. I tried to drive the thoughts from my mind, but I couldn't."

She confessed, "Many times those weren't dreams. I did come to you in your mind even though father forbade it. I couldn't resist."

"Oh."

"That's all you can say is oh? I risked my father's wrath and that's all you can say?" She teased.

"Somehow I don't think your father could stay mad at you very long."

Smiling, she leaned over and kissed him. They awoke the next morning in love's embrace.

Muirios revealed, "My master lives in a remote village that is a 5 day journey into the interior. We will leave within the hour."

Muireann warned, "I wish you would reconsider this journey. I feel that it will end in calamity."

He pleaded, "Please, I must do this."

Without any further discussion, the couple left.

Locating his former master wasn't difficult. The welcome was lukewarm. After dinner, Muireann excused herself to rest after the rigors of their journey.

His former master spoke first, "She seems like a fine wife, but…"

"But what?"

Hesitating, his former master revealed, "She's a…Selkie! And she's pregnant with twins! How long have you been in this Teltown Marriage?"

Muirios confessed, "About a week. I know she's a Selkie and she's pregnant. How did you know?"

Wagging his finger back and forth in a scolding motion he replied, "My dear apprentice, did you already forget that I am a master? It is my place to know and I have my ways."

Holding up his adder stone he peered into Muirios' bag, "You have her seal skin! What is that sword and other object?"

He replied, "The sword is a gift from her father as well as the gold and silver adder stone. The sealskin is Muireann's gift."

His former master scolded, "There is danger and heartbreak in the love of a Selkie. To make matters worse, you're bringing half Selkie children into the world. What happens when the call of their mother and the sea causes them to abandon you? My advice is to give her sealskin back and let her return to the sea with your unborn children. I can arrange for a new wife that would be better suited for someone like yourself. One that looks to the future and all that it holds."

"I can't believe what I'm hearing! I love Muireann and will not leave her or send her away! Even if I loose it all in the future, I WILL enjoy the present. We thank you for the meal and lodging. We will leave in the early light so we can still part as friends," Muirios retorted.

Before his former master could say any more, Muirios left the room to join his wife and lover. She held and comforted him through the night.

In the stillness of the early morning, his former master opened the couple's bags in search of the sealskin. He had to save his former apprentice from the horrible fate that awaited him. Startled by a noise from behind, he turned just in time to see the blade of Fragarach cleave him in half. Muireann wiped the blood from the blade using his clothing.

She declared to the corpse, "It is the WILL of the Gods that we are together! NO man will separate us!"

Muirios awoke to the sickening sound of his master's death. Muireann had just returned to their room after replacing the sword in his bag.

"What was that sound! What have you done!"

She defended, "Protecting us and the future generations. Your former master sold himself to the new religion. He wanted to separate us. I can't allow that. I have waited too long to be with you."

"What did you do?"

"Nothing can resist the blade of Fragarach," she replied.

Muirios ran past her and into the hallway almost tripping over the corpse of his former master.

"NO! It wasn't suppose to be this way!"

Frantically, he rushed around gathering their belongings.

"We have to leave right now! If they find him, we will die!"

Trying to calm him, she replied, "You should be a little quieter or they will find him and us."

Banging on the front door interrupted their exchange. His former master's neighbors had heard the early morning commotion and were concerned.

"Are you all right? Are you hurt? Open the door so we can see!"

Muirios and Muireann left through the bedroom window in the predawn light.

Not long afterwards, the neighbors burst through the front door and found the corpse of his former master.

"Summon the soldiers and the inquisitors," one of the men barked.

Examining the grisly scene, the head inquisitor proclaimed, "This is disturbing indeed."

After a pause, he questioned, "Who were his guests?"

One of the neighbors offered, "His former apprentice and his new bride."

"Where are they now?"

Another answered, "We don't know, but they came here on foot."

The head inquisitor nodded to the captain. The cavalrymen mounted their horses and raced out of town in search of the criminals.

The inquisitor continued to question the neighbors, "Where does this apprentice live?"

"The northern most islands. His father and sister raised him. Some say his sister entertained Selkies and even became one. Others say they were killed years ago. In truth, little is known about him and even less about his new bride."

Three horsemen closed on the couple. This would be an easy take down. Muirios retrieved Fragarach from his bag and stood to face the horsemen as he pushed Muireann behind some rocks. The first horseman rushed in with his lance aimed at Muirios. Sidestepping the lance, Muirios cleaved the rider and horse in half. The remaining horsemen charged him at the same time. Muirios cut down a standing dead tree knocking both riders from their mounts. The men drew their swords and closed on him. When the duo was close enough, Muirios circled around with Fragarach extended cutting through his aggressor's amour and cleaving them in half.

Grabbing her hand, he helped Muireann upon a horse. Mounting the other horse, they raced off for his former home. By the time they reached his home, the inquisitors had posted a large reward for the capture of the couple and the soldiers were scouring the land for the outlaws.

As the couple was preparing to leave, a large group approached the house.

Muirios started to draw Fragarach, but his wife stayed him.

He challenged, "What is this about?"

One of the group responded, "We've heard you've taken a stand against the new religion and the church has a bounty on your heads. We also heard you're one of the last Druids in the region."

He admitted, "Yes. This is true. What are your intentions?"

Another of the group answered, "We have been branded outlaws too because we won't forsake the old ways and embrace the new religion. We would like to journey with you and establish a new home for those that embrace the old ways."

Muirios replied, "I only know that I'm heading north. I've heard of a large island to the far north that might be a suitable for such a venture."

Muireann revealed, "I know of this island and can guide us there. The Danes and their kind frequent it, but I'm sure a business agreement can be established. They are resisting the wave of the new religion in their lands too."

Muirios instructed, "We sail with the tide this evening."

The sea God, Albion sent his Selkie army into the rivers and lakes to hamper the soldier's advance. When the navy tried to leave their port in pursuit of the rag tag fleet, he sent great waves, lightening, and winds to batter the fleet. Many ships and men were lost and the commander was turned back in disgrace.

Muirios and his men reached their new home and established a business agreement with the Danes and their kindred. In just a season, the entire region prospered. Muirios and his queen, Muireann were highly favored. She delivered their twins and all was well between them.

One day, visitors from Muirios' old homeland came to propose a treaty. They had just returned from a mission to the Danes and had heard of the emerging kingdom to the north. The church had sent them to open relations with the new kingdom. While they had lived among the Danes, they had participated in the sport of seal hunting and acquired the taste for smoked seal meat.

Unaware of the prohibition in the new kingdom, they presented Muirios and his queen with fine sealskins and barrels of smoked seal meat. Muireann immediately recognized the skins and meat from her Selkie children. In a rage she grabbed the king's sword, Fragarach and cut off all seven of the heads from the emissaries.

Gathering the heads, she held them high and declared, "View the faces of evil, our ENEMIES! I declare that from this day forth, NO seal hunting ship or hunter will be safe from attack!"

Throwing the heads into the crowd, she rushed out of the room crying hysterically. Muirios rushed after her. Finally, he caught her in the courtyard.

"What are you doing! This will be seen as an act of war!"

She protested, "Those were my Selkie children!"

The weight of the revelation and of Muirios' position was unbearable. He fell to his knees sobbing, holding his distressed wife. He was a Druid King. As such, he had to pass judgment and ensure compliance. His wife's actions dictated she be executed and financial compensation be offered to the offended parties.

He couldn't he kill the love of his life and his children's mother! Muireann could read his thoughts and was even more distressed over the dilemma.

An angry mob burst from great hall demanding swift action. Muirios tried to explain, but was shouted down by the group. They started forward to seize Muireann, but Muirios produced Fragarach. Most of the group had seen Fragarach in action and knew there was no victory against it.

They accused, "You wrongfully defend a criminal! This is hypocrisy!"

He retorted, "I defend my wife, lover, and the mother of my children!"

"Things are not as they appear," Muirios added.

The group didn't understand, "Yes, the emissaries violated the law against the seal, but our law doesn't provided for execution except in cases where the guilty are caught in the act within our own country!"

"You will have to trust me on this. I will resolve the situation!"

Knowing they couldn't prevail against Fragarach and Muirios had always dealt fairly in all cases, the group dispersed.

Helping Muireann up, he held her for an hour.

After she calmed, she requested, "Please return my sealskin."

"No! I can't! You'll leave!"

"It's the only way to resolve this issue. I'll leave and you can tell them I was banished."

He knew she was right, but he didn't want her to leave.

"What about the children?"

"They will stay with their father. Each year at the Alban Heruin, bring them to the Eye of the Water Dragon where we can be together. You and I can spend the eve and night of Alban Heruin together." When the children are older, they can decide their path."

"I couldn't last a week without you. How will I endure a year?" Muirios lamented.

"I feel the same, but I see no other way," she comforted.

"We could all become Selkies."

"No. The path between this world and the Otherworld is at the convergence of the land, sea, and sky. As keeper of the old ways, you must occupy the land, I must occupy the sea, and our children will occupy the sky."

"What of our Teltown Marriage?"

"Just because our time is up in three days doesn't mean it has to end," she answered.

"Has it almost been a year and a day already?"

"Yes," she replied.

The couple made preparations to honor the Alban Heruin at the Eye of the Water Dragon. After spending their final two nights together, in the early glow of the predawn, Muirios handed his wife her sealskin. After kissing her two newborns goodbye and holding her husband in an embrace to last a year, she draped her sealskin over her shoulder and walked into the sea. Transforming into a seal, she disappeared beneath the waves.

With a heavy heart, her husband returned with the infants. He was inconsolable for many days. His wife had a tearful reunion with her father.

In the early evening hours, she came to her lover in his dreams. He could feel the fire of her touch and her soft lips. In love's embrace, he wrestled with his Selkie lover until the dawn of a new day chased away the shadows of the night.

The owl is the messenger between the Otherworld and our world. It symbolizes death, renewal, wisdom, magick, clairvoyance, and seeing what most can't or won't. The owl can see clearly and fly silently in the dark. It is a fascinating and sacred animal. The story of Blodeuwedd is a favorite tale for many.

Blodeuwedd's tale is very deep. She is a shape shifting goddess and one of the many faces of Sovereignty. Sovereignty is how the Celts think of the Lady, the spirit, the planetary energy, that which lives and moves and holds our being. Blodeuwedd's story is of the enabler.

She is the woman who teaches the young and heedless boy responsibility ... which is what Gwydion asks of her when he asks her to become his son's wife. Gwydion, the Master Enchanter of Britain, asks her to help his wastrel son, Llew Llaw Gyffes, become a worthy guardian and king for the Land of Gwynedd. She agrees. In order to do this she asks him to make a form to embody her, for her work in Middleworld for she is a spirit being with no solid shape in the everyday world except her totem, the owl. Gwydion does this by taking nine flowers and making a body to house her spirit.

Allen Hartley

Not of father, nor of mother was my blood, my body.
I was spellbound by Gwydion, prime enchanter of the Britons,
When he formed me from nine blossoms,
Nine buds of various kinds:
From primrose of the mountain,
Broom, meadow-sweet and cockle,
Together intertwined,
From bean in its shade-bearing
A white spectral army of earth, and earthly kind,
From blossoms of the nettle, oak, thorn and bashful chestnut
Nine powers of nine flowers,
Nine powers in me combined,
Nine buds of plant and tree.
Long and white are my fingers
As the ninth wave of the sea.

He makes a body for the goddess so that she can work effectively in Middleworld. Once embodied, she initiates Llew into the mysteries of kingship and being guardian to the goddess then, once her job is done, Blodeuwedd returns to her totem form, the owl, the Queen of the Night.

Trees of the Goddess

Water has always held a sacred place in my life and those of our ancestors. Water was a mysterious force to the Celts. Rivers were borders between this world and the Otherworlds. The mythical islands inhabited by the Fae and the Túatha Dé Danann were believed to be hidden under the sea or under lakes. Offerings to the gods were thrown into rivers and holy wells to ensure their entrance into the Otherworlds. Water from holy wells sprang forth from deep within the earth, connecting them to the Underworld and the realm of the ancestors.

Breac à linne, slat à coille is fiadh à fireach - mèirle às nach do ghabh gàidheal riamh nàire.

A fish from the river, a staff from the wood and a deer from the mountain - thefts no Gael was ever ashamed of.

The shoreline also represents a magickal boundary, constantly shifting like the tide, between this world and the Otherworld. For the Druids and Celts, the sea is one of the ways of approach to the Otherworld.

Mine are the waters of the womb, tears shed in joy and sadness, the healing waters that wash away the old and bring new beginnings. I am the mother of the world, my essence flows in the waters of all rivers, in the ebb and flow of the sea. Many are my names. I am Danu, the River Mother, the Great Mother of Gods and Men, the Divine Waters of Heaven that birthed life out of darkness.

Stephanie Woodfield

In the Celtic "Green World", there are guides that reveal passageways to the Otherworld. The Otherworld consists of the higher planes encompassing the mental and spiritual. The physical body resides in the physical plane. In the Celtic view, everything is encompassed in the physical, mental, and spiritual. This includes the animals, plants, rocks, trees, everything.

Waterfalls are sacred places that hold access to the Otherworld. Over a period of time, the waterfall will erode its base until a cave is formed. These allow one to enter the Otherworld. Many seek answers, others to enhance their magickal powers, yet others thrill at the journey into the unknown.

Certain animals serve as guides and liaisons between the physical world and the Otherworld. The blackbird, known by the

Gaelic Name as Druid Dhubh (Druid-doo) or "black druid" is one of the guides to the Otherworld.

The blackbird sings at twilight and later. Twilight and predawn are considered the time of transition from one reality to the next. The veil between the worlds is the thinnest, allowing entry into the Otherworld. It is a time of mental and spiritual awakening, a time to journey without our physical bodies to seek enlightenment and other gifts our ancestors and others that inhabit the Otherworld are willing to bestow upon us.

Pools and wells were also important to our Celtic ancestors. There is a deep place, far from any road or path, absent on any map and hidden from mortal eyes, which reach down into the very beginnings of time. Flowing upward from the vast depths comes all the waters of the world. Trickling between the roots of the great hazelnut trees, which stand in a solemn circle at the wells edge, the waters come together and give birth to the many rivers of Ireland and eventually, the sea.

Finnegas and the Salmon of Knowledge

Long ago, a single salmon made the long journey inland from the sea and found itself swimming alone in that great dark pool. Hungry from its exertions and finding nothing else to eat, the salmon consumed nine hazelnuts which had dropped one by one from each of the trees surrounding the well. Taking nourishment as they do, from the undiluted waters, which spring from the center of existence, these trees bear fruit of amazing potency. In this way a simple fish was imbued with both immortality and the knowledge of all things.

Years passed and the legend of the Salmon of Knowledge spread to the mortal men who came and settled in Ireland. Many sought to catch the magical fish, knowing that to taste its flesh would convey unto them the knowledge of all things. One of these men, a great Druid and poet, learned that a large salmon, pale almost to white with age, had been seen swimming in a pool of water at the edge of the river Boyne.

For six years he lived at the edge of that pool, waiting with his nets for the moment when he would catch a glimpse of his prize. Finally the moment came for him to cast his net over the water. The salmon was his at last! Wading back to the shore, he handed the fish to his student, a loyal and trustworthy young lad, with instructions on how it should be prepared.

While the old man made himself ready for the long overdue feast, the fish was skewered and suspended over a fire. Turning the fish on its spit, a drop of hot oil ran down the skewer and seared the lad's thumb. Burned and in pain, the young man naturally sucked his thumb. Through no fault of his own he had disobeyed his master and tasted the cooking fish.

Returning to his camp, the Druid could smell the savory aroma of cooking fish. Pausing for a moment to look into the eyes of his pupil, he saw there an intelligence he had never before known. With a sigh, he offered the fish to his student. The Salmon of Knowledge had eluded him yet again.

Water features can help us balance our physical, mental, and spiritual aspects. It can be the rushing of a great river or the quiet lazy flow of a stream beneath the trees. With a large percentage of our physical bodies composed of water, it is not hard to understand our physical attraction to water. Water speaks to our souls and invites us to explore the other aspects of our lives.

Rivers are roads which move, and which carry us whither we desire to go.

Blaise Pascal

Chapter 7
Magick

Magick is the projection of the will, resulting in creation. Creation of chaos, curses, order, clairvoyance, protection, judgment, life forms, knowledge, and greater magick. Magick is a tool to gain greater knowledge, wisdom, and powers. As with much of our ancestral knowledge, magickal knowledge and practices have been polluted, obscured, and trivialized by those that want to control the masses. The puppet masters want exclusive use of magick. Magick is intended to advance users during their multiple life journeys, not control others.

The Bind Rune for magick is composed of eight Runes. Each Rune contains an aspect for the projection of the will. Projection of the will expands the soul and its energies. Repeated projections allow us to become more powerful. Upon reaching certain levels, the veil that obscures the knowledge of our past lives is burned off. Travel between the dimensions and iterations is possible.

Üruz/Úr ᚢ is the base Rune of the magick Bind Rune. It is used to draw and project energies. Repeated use increases the amount of energy that can be drawn and projected, increasing the reserves of the magickal user. Üruz/Úr represents the cycles of our iterations – birth, life, and death. It is the Rune of courage, boldness, freedom, and rebellion. It provides the user with the strength to stand apart from the masses, venturing down the path of higher planes of existence. As with all things, those that embrace Üruz/Úr must take responsibility for their actions and destiny. It's not for the timid, those that can't bear the bright light of accountability, or the devious. A balance must be maintained when magickal operations are used. If it isn't, the dimensional universe will forcibly balance the situation. An exchange of "gifts" is always required in magickal operations. It's not a process of "free handouts", but a balanced relationship.

Thurisaz/þurs ᚦ is the Rune of regeneration and birth, transformation and life, and death. The powers of this Rune are wild, a strong will is required to direct it. Üruz/Úr is used to transfer energies to Thurisaz/þurs, manifesting the will of the magickal user. It can be used in magickal operations to raise and guide thunderstorms and lightning. Thurisaz/þurs also represents the thorn, which is used in magick to cause a stasis in the intended. Odin used a magickal thorn from the tree of sleep to cause the battle maiden, Brynhild to sleep.

Youngest of all the battle-maidens was Brynhild. Nevertheless, to her, Odin All-Father had shown more of the Runes of Wisdom than he had shown to any of her sisters. When the time came for Brynhild to journey down into Midgard he gave her a swan-feather dress such as he had given before to the three Valkyrie sisters— Alvit, Olrun, and Hladgrun. In the dazzling plumage of a swan the

young battle-maiden flew down from Asgard. She had not yet gone to the battlefields, waters drew her. As she waited on the will of the All-Father, she sought out a lake that had golden sands for its shore and as a maiden, bathed in it.

There dwelt near the lake a young hero whose name was Agnar. One day, as Agnar lay by the lake, he saw a swan with dazzling plumage fly down to it. While she was in the reeds, the swan-feather dress slipped off her. Agnar beheld the swan change to a maiden. So bright was her hair, so strong and swift were all her movements, that he knew her for one of Odin's battle-maidens; for one of those who give victory and choose the slain. Very daring was Agnar, he set his mind upon capturing this battle-maiden, even though he should bring on himself the wrath of Odin. He hid the swan-feather dress that she had left in the reeds so when she came out of the water, she might not fly away. Agnar gave back to her the swan-feather dress, but she had to promise that she would be his battle-maiden.

As they talked together, the young Valkyrie saw in him a hero that one from Asgard might help. Very brave and very noble was Agnar. Brynhild went with him as his battle-maiden and she told him much from the Runes of Wisdom that she knew. She showed him that the All-Father's last hope was in the bravery of the heroes of the earth; with the Chosen from the Slain for his Champions he would make battle in defense of Asgard.

Always, Brynhild was with Agnar's battalion. Above the battles she hovered, her bright hair and flashing battle-dress outshining the spears and swords and shields of the warriors. The gray-beard King Helmgunnar made war on the young Agnar. Odin favored the gray-beard King and to him he promised the victory. Brynhild knew the will of the All-Father, but to Agnar, not to Helmgunnar she gave the victory.

Doomed was Brynhild on the instant she went against Odin's will. Never again might she come into Asgard. A mortal woman she was now and the Norns began to spin the thread of her mortal destiny. Sorrowful was Odin All-Father that the wisest of his battle-maidens might never appear in Asgard nor walk by the benches at the feasts of his Champions in Valhalla.

He rode down on Sleipner to where Brynhild was. When he came before her, it was his, not her head that was bowed down. She knew now that the World of Men was paying a bitter price for the strength that Asgard would have in the last battle. The bravest and noblest were being taken from Midgard to fill up the ranks of Odin's Champions. Brynhild's heart was full of anger against the rulers of Asgard and she cared no more to be of them.
Odin looked on his unflinching battle-maiden, and he said, "Is there aught thou wouldst have me bestow on thee in thy mortal life, Brynhild?"

Brynhild answered, "Naught save this, that in my mortal life no one but a man without fear, the bravest hero in the world, may claim me for wife."

All-Father bowed his head in thought, "It shall be as thou hast asked, only he who is without fear shall come near thee."

Then on the top of the mountain that is called Hindfell, he had a Hall built that faced the south. Ten Dwarfs built it of black stone. When the Hall was built, he put round it a wall of mounting and circling fire. Odin All-Father took a thorn of the Tree of Sleep and put it into the flesh of the battle-maiden. With her helmet on her head and the breast-mail of the Valkyrie upon her, he lifted Brynhild in his arms and carried her through the wall of mounting and circling fire. He laid her upon the couch that was within the Hall. There she would lie in slumber until the hero who was without fear should ride through the flame and waken her to the life of a mortal woman. He took farewell of her and rode back to Asgard on Sleipner. He might not foresee what fate would be hers as a mortal woman. The fire he had left went mounting and circling around the Hall that the Dwarfs had built. For ages that fire would be a fence around where Brynhild, once a Valkyrie, lay in sleep.

The Children of Odin
The Book of Northern Myths

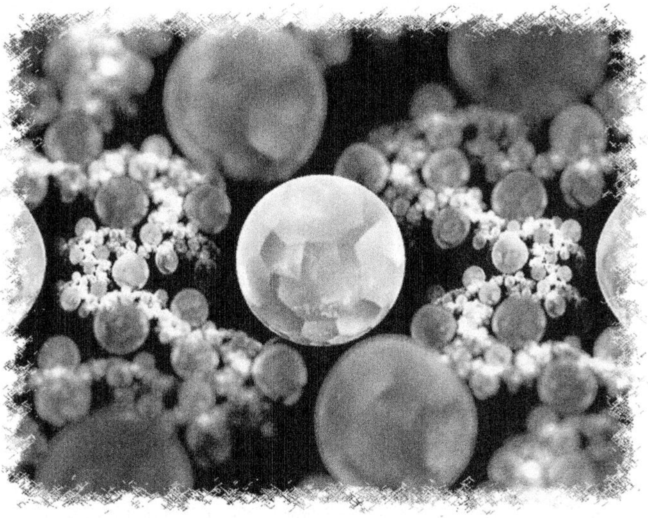

ANSUZ/Óss ᚨ is the Rune of the spoken word that projects the will. Using the vibrational energies created by speech, magick is created and projected. Advance users project magick from the vibrations of the soul, without vocalization. Advanced forms of life communicate telepathically. Humans have this ability, but most people are taught to ignore it or that it is evil. The resulting weakness blinds humans to the numerous conversations that are happening all around them. That "dumb dog" isn't as dumb as you think. If humans lived on the higher planes of the animals and plants, this world would be much different.

If we could walk with the animals, talk with the animals... Dr. Doolittle

Gebo/Gjöf X represents the Rune of giving and sacrifice, freely giving of ourselves or something of value as a gift. It also represents personal sacrifice to gain wisdom, knowledge, and power. Odin sacrificed himself to gain the knowledge of the Runes.

Odin's Rune Song

I know myself hanging on the wind cold tree for nine icy nights.
Wounded by the spear, consecrated to Wodan
I consecrated to myself.
I was hanging on the mighty tree which conceals man
Where man grew out of its roots.

They offered me neither bread nor wine
So I bent down in search.
I recognized the Runes; wailing I grasped them.
Until I sank down from the tree.

Now I began to increase, to be wise,
To grow and to feel well.
From the word, word grew after word
And deed shaped to deeds with deeds.

Now I know the songs like no wise one knows
And none of the children of men.
And should these songs, o human child, be un-learnable to you for
Sheer endless time;
Grasp them as you get hold of them, use them as you hear of them.
Hail you if you retain them!

Runes you will find, and readable staves,
Very strong staves,
Very stout staves,
Staves that Bolthor stained,
Made by mighty powers,
Graven by the prophetic God.

For the Gods by Odin, for the Elves by Dain,
By Dvalin, too, for the Dwarves,
By Asvid for the hateful Giants,
And some I carved myself:
Thund, before man was made, scratched them,
Who rose first, fell thereafter.

Know how to cut them,
Better not to ask than to over-pledge
As a gift that demands a gift.
Better not to send
Than to slay too many...

Jera/Ár ᛋ represents the cycling of energy. These cycles can be influenced, projected, and redirected through the will. Everything has a cycle. Our time in this iteration – birth, life, and death are a cycle known to all. Other cycles such as seasonal and water cycles are prominent in this existence. The cycling of energies is known as vibrational energies. The projection of the will raises or diminishes vibrational energies. Cycling energies surround us and are available to all that can perceive and respectfully work with them.

Our ancient ancestors understood these principles. Through programmatic revision and removal of our ancestral knowledge, prohibitions on exploring the powers within our souls by religious leaders, and laziness, many have been turned into magickal weaklings/sheeple. The easier for the puppet masters to control.

Many of those that venture down the magickal path of our ancestors are provided with the placebo of polluted magickal practices that are ineffective and "harmless" – just what the puppet masters wanted. It takes a strong soul to stand apart and walk on the true magickal path. It is a journey of many lifetimes.

Those that cling to the sheeple path of religious programs are deprived of their TRUE spiritual energies and their soul is left malnourished. We chose to return to this iteration to expand our knowledge and powers – expand the power of our soul. We knew before we came this would not be any easy iteration and many would fail.

Nothing rests; everything moves; everything vibrates.

The Kybalion

Sowilo/Sól ᛋ is the Rune of the Sun, invincibility, and final triumph. Sowilo/Sól is the lightening bolt that activates the energies of the soul and other Runes that are used conjunction with it. It can be used as a shielding or combative Rune. Combined with Thurisaz/þurs and Üruz/Úr, NOTHING can resist the energies they generate. A strong soul is required to intertwine and direct these energies. Jera/Ár is used to cycle up these energies and rebalance them after they have been directed by the will. These energies were used to create our worlds and those that inhabit them – EVERYTHING that inhabits them. Using these energies enhances the powers of our souls. The purpose of our journey in this iteration is to enhance our soul and ascend to the next level of our progression. So many have been side tracked with other interests and their souls drained by those that would enslave them. The puppet masters use the energies of other souls for their own progression. It takes great effort to stand on your own and advance the soul.

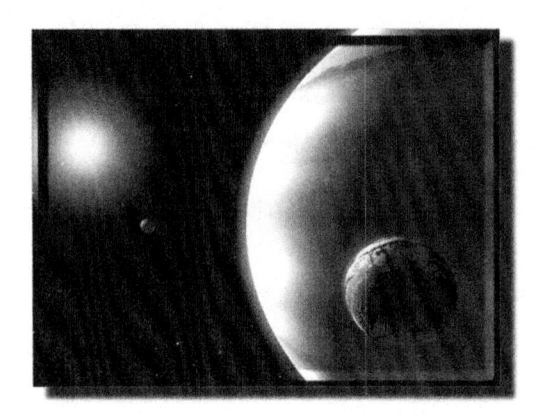

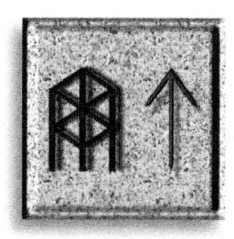

Tiwaz/Týr ↑ is the Rune of justice. It instills courage and honor as a result of true justice being administered. There are those, which have passed through multiple iterations, having their souls refined through testing and trials that are given the responsibilities and powers to judge matters and situations. When the system is polluted through corruption, favoritism, and self interest, the honor is lost. The masses are reduced to sheeple, not having the courage to stand against the perverted system. As with all things, a balance has to be maintained. The dimensional universe will insert a strong soul with the abilities and powers to restore the honor and true justice.

Our ancient ancestors looked to the Druids to hear and judge all matters, enforce judgments, provide training, maintain ancestral history, and societal structure. The church violently crushed our ancestor's society and degraded them to sheeple, blindly following only church sanctioned leaders. The Druids and others that resisted the church were brutally exterminated, replacing our ancestor's society of strong individualism and self reliance with a mindless, dependent one, based on the whims and agendas of the church leaders. Over the centuries, the strong souls of our ancestors have returned to prepare the way for the full restoration of the old ways.

Magick is used to defend against another's attack or to carry out a judgment. This is a serious matter and should be justified. Magick is very powerful however it's used. Misuse of Magick brings dishonor to the wielder and fear to the masses. Justified use brings honor to the wielder, providing courage and inspiration to the society.

The Druid Dhubh (Druid-doo or Dark Druid)

For months I heard disturbing reports of the violent push into the lands of our ancestors by the leaders and followers of the new religion. A religion not based on sound logic or principles, but the whims of power hungry men with designs to force the masses into servitude. As with all unjust campaigns, the elite leadership and their favored puppets were exempted from the burden of following the edicts they established.

More disturbing were the reports of the current leaders in our society that exchanged the compliance and the subservience of their people for favors and positions granted by the new religion.

I shifted to my black wulf form and raced through the alpine forest. My target was the new leader that had been inserted by the church into a community not too far from my secluded dwelling. The new leader was from the lands far south of our borders, across many seas. He harshly enforced the programs of the church upon our people. In hypocrisy, he didn't follow the teachings of the new religion, but embraced his own desires. The people weren't accustomed to this manner of behavior from a leader. The soldiers of the church attached the freshly burnt heads of the former community leaders to long poles for all to see.

The new leader declared, "Let this be a lesson to all, deviation from my laws or those of the church will be punished with a horrible death. A death not only for the offender, but all of their family."

After allowing the seriousness of the situation to register with the masses, he continued, "I understand there are others among you that have magickal powers and knowledge, others that you look to for leadership and judgment."

Pointing to the charred heads, he prodded, "These were local community leaders. I want to know where to find the wise ones and those called Druids."

After a long silence, he proposed, "We can do this the easy way…Or we can do it the hard way."

He nodded to the three hooded men in the corner. The trio pushed their noisy cart to the center of the gathering and bowed to the new leader.

"I want to introduce a special group of men trained by the church to extract ANY information I need. Even information you didn't know you had. These men can keep you alive by the grace and miracles of our god, your new god, to inflict additional pain and suffering until you die or confess."

After a few tense moments, the new leader continued, "If no one has any information to willingly offer, perhaps we can start with a few of the young maidens. Surely they've heard where these people can be found."

Responding to his nod, the hooded men entered the crowd and seized three of the young women. They were like wildcats kicking, hitting, and punching their captors. One of the hooded men slapped his captive. In response, she drew a secreted blade, cutting off his ear and slashed his cheek. He released her to stop the gushing blood from the side of his head and face. The woman stabbed him in the eye and slashed his throat. The backside of a soldier's blade sent her into darkness.

Furious, the new leader declared, "That one will be publicly punished and burned at the stake along with her family. An attack on the officials of the church is punishable by death."

In my wulf form, I jumped forward, driving the new leader to the ground. Leaping from his back, I ripped the throats from the two remaining hooded men. The captives grabbed their unconscious friend and raced back into the crowd. As the soldiers encircled me, great waves of internal pain racked their bodies causing them to fall to the ground. I raced past the soldiers and stood over the new leader.

He shook with fear, but in defiance demanded, "Who are you to interfere with official church business? I'll send you to hell's flames and banish your soul from heaven!"

Transforming into my human form I stood before him, "I neither fear your threats nor recognize the church. It was formed by men to deceive and control the masses. You offer NOTHING but mindless slavery to all that embrace the new religion. That includes those that bargain for your favors in return for the submission of themselves and their people."

I could hear the whisperings from the crowd behind me, "Druid Dhubh, Dark Druid."

The new leader slowly rose to his feet, "You don't scare me! You're a pretender that have all the people scared and blindly submitting to your will."

I just smiled and nodded to my dark companion standing in the corner. With a glare fixed on the new leader, she slowly advanced his direction. Her energies were so great he had to retreat a step or two.

I introduced my companion, "This is Hekate, queen of all the wise ones, the Otherworld, and our world. She is also known as Morrigan, Isis, Inanna, Brigid, Badb, Sekhemt, and many other names."

"I'm known as Druid Dhubh, the Dark Druid, or Dark Wulf. You wished to find us, all you had to do was ask. Hurting our people is NOT the way to find us. Unlike your god, we live among our people and consider their petitions."

The new leader retorted, "What do you want?"

"You were searching us out, so we appeared."

Looking at his soldiers he asked, "What have you done with my men?"

"They are no longer in this iteration. Hekate, great queen of the dead, magick, and the people has dispatched them to their next iteration."

After a pause, I continued, "I'm here to pass judgment. You have killed our appointed leaders and are attempting to subvert our established society. My judgment is final, the dimensional universe will acknowledge and honor it."

Dark are his Deeds, Skin, and Tongue
All will be undone
White is his Facade, to Placate
Trusting are the Sheeple, Beneath the Steeple
Hiding, his Schemes of Revenge
Using the Mold from Times of Old
He Lies and Instills Fear for those that Hear
His Twisted Words of Promised Protection

I extended my hand to the condemned and encouraged him to take the Rune staves I had carved and stained with the blood of another condemned soul.

After a moment he yanked them from my hand, "What are these?"

As he examined them, I explained, "The punishment for your crimes."

He retorted, "I can't read them!"

"They are powerful and sacred symbols that have existed before all that is."

Angrily he asked, "What do they say?"

"Your physical body and soul will be shredded and returned to cosmic dust, you'll cease to exist. You have a dark soul and have been marked inwardly and outwardly. This iteration was your last chance to rise above the deeds of the past."

"What deeds?"

I motioned to Hekate. She nodded to her apprentices. Two of the apprentices placed a large bronze stand and platter in front of the condemned. Using a bronze vase, a third apprentice poured water, drawn from a well at the base of an ancient oak tree into the platter. Hekate stepped forward and motioned for the condemned to stand on the other side of the platter. Speaking archaic words of power, Hekate held her hands above the water. As the waters began to churn, a bluish, green fog covered the surface. Hekate spoke more words of power and the center of the fog dissipated.

She commanded, "Look into the center, see your lives and all that you've done for ill or good."

As he looked, the veil covering his soul was rent. He was flooded with all the knowledge and memories from his past lives. It was painful! All the sorrow, pain, and oppression he had inflicted on others was turned back on his soul. Retching his gaze from the waters of the bronze platter he reeled about.

"You're a trickster, an imposter, a deceiver!"

Hekate mutely watched, which further angered the condemned.

Pointing his finger at me, "And you have NO authority to judge me!"

In anger he discarded the Rune staves into the nearby fire. They flashed vigorously, emitting a blinding light. The condemned screamed in pain as his body and soul decomposed to cosmic dust. The crowd watched with approval and fear. Hekate stepped forward, with a wave of her hand she summoned the wind to disperse the dusty remains as she and her trio of apprentices vanished from sight.

I addressed the crowd, "In eight days we'll have a full moon. I'll return at midnight to review the candidates that have been selected for your new leaders. From these, I'll make the final selection. Choose wisely."

Turning, I transformed into my black wulf form and raced off into the alpine forest.

Mannaz/Maður ᛗ is the Rune of logic, intellect, and knowledge. All are essential for effective magick or the projection of the will.

> I recognized the Runes; wailing I grasped them.
> Until I sank down from the tree.
>
> Now I began to increase, to be wise, to grow and
> To feel well. From the word, word grew after
> word and deed shaped to deeds with deeds.
>
> Now I know the songs like no wise one knows...
>
> Odin's Rune Song

The esoteric knowledge of the Runes have been obscured, fragmented, hidden, revised, and misunderstood for centuries. Some of this was done to protect the REAL knowledge of the Runes from the church and its agents. When the church targeted a region to assimilate, it would establish a mission for the purpose of documenting the area and its inhabitants. Detailed information was constructed about the beliefs, customs, relationships, language, and technology of the people. The information was used to create a palatable religious package for the region. Many of the indigenous practices and beliefs were incorporated into the package to make the people feel more comfortable with their conversion. The objective of the church was to create a submissive flock of sheeple that had total dependency on the church to direct EVERY activity in their lives.

Religious and secular leaders were also cataloged. These were approached first in conversion efforts. If that failed, they were eliminated and replaced with puppets that would comply with the church's directives.

Before they were eliminated, those with special knowledge were tortured in an effort to obtain it. To protect the sacred knowledge of the Runes and other secrets, some of the masters altered them.

Adding to the complexity, many of the societies had commercial and social exchanges with each other. Part of the exchanges included goods, services, customs, knowledge, religious beliefs, and technology. As a result, there are multiple Runic systems, but the Elder Futhark is the original. The church has dismissed all the Runic systems as alphabets used for writing. They don't want anyone but themselves to have special power or knowledge.

Unlike other languages, there doesn't appear to be a grammar rule set to accompany the Runic writing system. Even though the characters have been assigned alpha and phonetic values, the sacred symbols have always existed and are vibrated on a higher plane with the soul.

Souls have been returning with extensive knowledge of the Runes from previous lives for the express purpose of restoring the true knowledge of the Runes. This knowledge is available to all who will open their souls and listen.

Using the Rune Perthro/Perð ᚲ the knowledge and secrets of the Runes can be discovered through meditation and assistance from the Otherworld. This won't happen overnight, it will require a great deal of research and study, practice, and quiet meditation. Your soul will have to be cleared of all the clutter that inundates us in an effort to distract and interfere with our purpose of returning to this iteration, to advance our souls to higher levels of knowledge and power.

When the ears of the student are ready to hear, then cometh the lips to fill them with Wisdom.

The Kybalion

Chapter 8
Warriors and Weapons

Deep in the sacred chamber, I stand on a black marble platform above an opening to the primal abyss. My soul reaches for its depths, drawing the raw energies into the chamber. Energies used to create all that has ever existed. Respectfully, I call to my companions.

I've accomplished the first part of my tasking, now it's time to finish the task and rid ourselves of an eternal enemy. Blue mists rise from the depths of the abyss as my companions answer. They take shape at the entrances of the eight halls.

Enki steps forward and queries, "What news of your task?"

I respond, "Great Enki, I've battled our foe through countless iterations and have once again separated her soul from her body. It's time to execute her judgment, shredding her soul and returning it to cosmic dust. She has proven herself MOST unworthy of existing in this dimensional universe."

The group agreed with the judgment. We left the sacred chamber and appeared at the rear of a chapel conducting her funeral. Murmurs and whispers followed our group as we advanced down the aisle for a final viewing of our enemy. As we approached, a flood of memories filled my soul. She was a very cunning and capable one. I could still feel her soul, it was near.

Moving quickly from a corner, she exclaimed, "I knew you'd come!"

Abruptly, she halted as I opened my hand over her corpse to reveal a black stone with blood stained Runes. As I dropped the stone on her remains, she rushed at me screaming. Her body and soul was shredded to cosmic dust.

The officials were alarmed at the situation. They had seen her body instantly turn to dust, but they didn't understand what happened. The guests in the front rows also witnessed the events, panic raced through the room. My honored companion, Hekate lowered her hood and held her hands up for silence.

"This vile soul has been judged and is NOT worthy to continue in future iterations. After progressing to high levels of achievement through multiple iterations, she has chosen to abuse her powers to enslave, afflict, and inhibit the growth of other souls. This is the path of her master, our ancient adversary. She chose, like you to follow this path. You're all judged unworthy to continue in future iterations by your attitudes and actions. You've supported the actions of this unworthy one and continue to embrace the path of our adversary."

The crowd was furious and became unruly. I held out my hand and displayed another black stone emblazed with blood stained Runes. Levitating the stone, I projected it into the center of the room. Gathering energies from the depths of the abyss, I directed them into the stone. Great waves of vibrational energy raced through the room shredding the bodies and souls of all present.

Walking past the ashes, we departed. From a wooded hillside overlooking the chapel, I summoned a great vortex of energy. It swept away the building, its contents, and the past. Our group returned to the sacred chamber and parted.

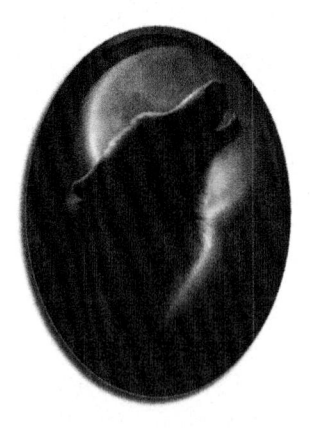

The valor that struggles is better than the weakness that endures.

Hegel

Our Celtic heritage is a cross pollination and synthesization of multiple groups of people. Depending on the snapshot in time used to examine the Celts, the kaleidoscope of the culture is ever changing. As with many cultures, not all the warriors were of the martial ranks. There are many powerful ones with weapons and abilities beyond the sword and spear - weapons of magick. There are some that are part of both the martial and magickal ranks, brandishing magickal and physical weapons. Many times, there are alliances between the warriors and magickal users. The most important thing in the Celtic society was providing for and protecting yourself, your family, and those you had pledged allegiances. If you couldn't help or protect yourself, how could you expect to help others?

This is very true today. The concept of self reliance and responsibility is contrary to the sociopathic views of the puppet masters and their puppets. They loudly declare "they know what's best for you and will take care of all your needs." Through various programs, the puppet masters have dumbed down the masses and removed any motivation except to seek more hand outs and aid.

Be bold and mighty forces will come to your aid

Johann Wolfgang von Goethe

For many, our true Celtic heritage has been erased or edited. If we have knowledge or memories, it's usually an edited version. Most people associate Celtic with Irish or Scottish culture. It goes beyond and is greater than just the edited versions of the Irish, Scottish, and British histories.

We should be open to the whisperings and visions from our ancestors as we research and read the stories of the past. Many hardships can be avoided or overcome if we look to the lessons of the past.

What experience and history teaches us is that people and governments have never learned anything from history, or acted on principles deduced from it.

Hegel

Am fear nach gheidh na h-airm `nam na sith, Cha bhi iad aige 'n am a chogaidh.

Who keeps not his arms in times of peace, Will have no arms in times of war.

Gaelic Proverb

The Bind Rune for the warrior is composed of nine Runes symbolizing the characteristics of a warrior. It is similar in appearance to the Magick Bind Rune. Just as a powerful magickal user projects his will to create, the warrior uses his weapons and will to create. The physical projection of the will is used to enforce laws and edicts, protect the people, assist allies, and secure resources. The warrior also creates death from life, chaos from order, and crushes the hope of his enemy. The warrior also preserves life from death, order from chaos, and the hope of the people.

If blood will flow when flesh and steel are one
Drying in the color of the evening sun
Tomorrow's rain will wash the stains away
But something in our minds will always stay
Perhaps this final act was meant
To clinch a lifetime's argument
That nothing comes from violence
And nothing ever could
For all those born beneath an angry star
Lest we forget how fragile we are
On and on the rain will fall
Like tears from a star
On and on the rain will say
How fragile we are...

Sting

Üraz/Úr ᚢ is the first Rune of the warrior's Bind Rune. It represents the basis of a warrior – strength, endurance, boldness, and courage. These are the combined attributes of the soul and physical body. It represents the drawing and projection of energies. The warrior draws energies from the depths of his soul and projects them through his weapons. Projections of this type inflict serious harm to the opponent. Advanced warriors can project energies at their target without a physical weapon.

Am fear a thug buaidh air fhein, thug e buaidh air namhaid

He who conquers himself, conquers an enemy

Gaelic Proverb

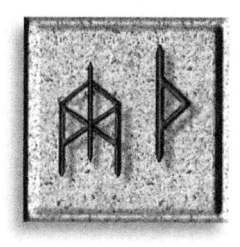

Thurisaz/Þorn ᚦ represents cutting, sharpness, pain, brute strength, destructive power, chaos, and ruin. It also represents death and regeneration. The energies of the Rune are wild like the Nordic Berserkers, a strong will is required to direct them.

One of the great stories from our Celtic heritage is the Battle of Bannockburn. Robert the Bruce, King of Scotland, invokes the energies of the warrior and defeats the larger, heavily armed English army under the direction of Edward II.

Never interrupt your enemy when he is making a mistake

Napoleon Bonaparte

On 23rd June 1314 by the river Bannockburn, Sir Henry de Bohun, a young English knight, made a fatal error of judgment. Wearing heavy armor and mounted on a war horse he pointed his lance in the direction of Robert the Bruce. Recklessly he charged, confident that he could win this 'little' battle by dispatching its leader before it even got started.

The Bruce was on a smaller horse, with not much more than a shield standing between Sir Henry's lance and his chest. But it meant he was also light of foot. As Sir Henry charged on him he steered his horse aside, stood up in his stirrups, and chopped his axe through Sir Henry's passing helmet. Sir Henry died almost as much of embarrassment as an axe-blow. So began the Battle of Bannockburn.

Bannockburn changed the face of military warfare and proved that heavily armored knights were no match for foot soldiers. In previous battles knights would meet with enemy knights and clash with each other on horseback. The foot soldiers were little more than servants to the feudal knights. They ran along behind mopping up unmentionables and lending support. They were armed of course, but not organized.

The Scottish army was made up of at least 7000 foot soldiers (exact numbers are unknown), many of whom had won their stripes in guerrilla warfare, ambushing and raiding the English militia who occupied Scotland. But they had only 600 mounted light-horsemen. The English were 3000-strong with heavily armored horsemen and 10,000 more on foot.

When Sir Robert Keith, leader of the 600 Scottish knights, climbed a hill to spy on the arriving English army the night before battle, what an alarming sight must have greeted him. Coats-of-arms and banners in every color; swords and shields glinting in the long evening shadows, and an insurmountable field of horses. Robert the Bruce, however, had a masterly plan.

William Wallace had begun the War of Independence that won back castle after castle, town after town for the Scottish. When he was executed for treason in 1305, Edward I regained control and all seemed lost. Then Robert the Bruce got the fire in his belly and re-instituted the same guerrilla strategies. He was crowned King of

Scotland at Scone in 1306, then in 1307 Edward I died, and Scotland heaved a sigh of relief. Some even threw parties.

Edward II had no stomach for the war his father had been so keen to wage. Immersed in personal battles at home he neglected his castles north of the border, and Robert's army took full advantage of that. One by one they fell to the Scottish.

Stirling Castle was one of the last remaining strongholds of English control. The Scottish laid siege to it for 4 months. In the end the castle's occupier, Sir Philip of Mowbray, did a deal with them. If reinforcements hadn't arrived from England by Midsummer's day 1314 (23rd June), he would call it a fair cop and hand over the castle.

Effectively Mowbray was calling for the English king to invade Scotland. He summoned his army of feudal knights, who didn't expect to face much of an opposition from that ragged band of Scottish guerrillas. Meanwhile Robert the Bruce made intricate preparations for the battle of his life.

Using Wallace's methodology he divided his troops into schiltrons, or units. Each schiltron was composed of a 'Crown formation' of close-knit foot soldiers with spears facing outwards, like a giant human hedgehog. He ordered pits dug on the north side of the Bannock and covered them with branches. More concealed pits were dug in front of the schiltrons.

He made sure the geography was on his side. If the English got across the Bannockburn they had to contend with marshes and the river Forth hemming them in. The only way to cross the Bannock directly to the battle ground was by a narrow ford. The English were forced to form themselves into a column to negotiate the ford, which gave the Scottish a clear advantage. The blood bath that ensued meant that the Scots won the field on the first day.

Morale was low that night in the English camp. A whole day of fighting and no ground won. Sir Alexander Seton, a Scot fighting on the English side, defected that night to the Scottish camp and told King Robert of the despondency of the English. They believed God was against them in this unholy war, and some regiments were rebelling, raiding the supplies and getting drunk, as it was likely to be their last night on Earth. In the shadow of Stirling Castle King Edward must have lain in a troubled sleep.

The next day the English decided to cross the Bannockburn further east and attack the schiltrons sideways. This was a disaster. The piece of land Edward chose to fight on was hemmed in by two rivers and impossibly boggy land.

One after another the Scottish schiltrons charged on the mounted knights. It soon became obvious who was going to win. The English king was led away and his army retreated in turmoil. Many were drowned in the river. Even the unassailable Welsh archers, Edward's pièce de résistance, were scattered by the Scottish cavalry. Robert the Bruce's superior military preparation meant victory belonged to the Scottish, along with Stirling Castle.

This battle was a major turning point in the war, which eventually ended in the treaty of Edinburgh-Northampton in 1328. Unfortunately this was broken by Edward III in 1333, inflaming a second and more complex war which finally died out in 1357.

Gebo/Gjöf ᚷ is the Rune of sacrifice and giving. The warrior offers the gifts of his service and life for his people. In the best case, the people acknowledge and recognize this sacrifice with memorials, awards, parades, and compensation. In the less fortunate cases the people are taught to despise and neglect the warrior, not recognizing or acknowledging the sacrifices that were made on their behalf. Gebo/Gjöf is also the Rune of Initiation and training, sacrifices made to obtain knowledge, power, and wisdom. The warrior has specialized training that can last for years. Many times, the training is so demanding that only a few will successfully finish. The way of the warrior isn't easy or a path for all and the demands are high. Even those that complete the training and spend a lifetime in the service of the people still pay a high price.

Na sir 's na seachainn an cath

Neither seek nor shun the fight

Gaelic Proverb

A few thousand years ago in western Scotland, lived a great warrior queen named Scathach. Her name meant "The Shadowy One." Scathach ran a training academy for young warriors.

The great Ulster warrior Cuchulainn was Scathach's most famous student. He sought her out because the father of the woman he wished to marry, Emer, had said they could not wed until Cuchulainn had been trained as a champion by Scathach. In this he was hoping to avoid giving his daughter to the hero, since it was notoriously difficult to find Scathach's island and survive her training course.

Through his bravery and strength Cuchulainn found his way there and used his famous "salmon leap" to gain access to her stronghold. He threatened her at sword point in order to persuade her to teach him everything she knew. She granted the young warrior three wishes, to instruct him properly, to grant him her daughter without bride price and to foretell his future.

She told him she foresaw a great and glorious career for him but did not see him living any longer than thirty years of age. Scathach did grant her daughter, Uathach, to Cuchulainn but it is said that she also lay with him. She taught him his art carefully and at the same time she taught the young warrior Ferdia, who became Cuchulainn's brother in arms. Both were educated to an equal level, but Scathach gave Cuchulainn one gift in secret. This was the legendary Gae Bolga, a spear which separated in to barbs on entering human flesh. Its first strike was always fatal. It was this weapon, which caused the death of Ferdia when the two men were forced to fight against each other in the saga of the Tain.

In return for this instruction, Cuchulainn stood against the enemies of Scathach led by the warrior queen, Aife. He saved the lives of Scathach's two sons and went into battle as her champion against Aife. He held a sword at Aife s throat and made her promise to give hostages to Scathach, to keep peace forever more, and to bear him a son. This Aife did and Cuchulainn returned to Scathach to rest after his great deeds. He left her island after seven years fully trained in the arts of war and was famed as the greatest warrior Ireland has ever known as a result of her teaching.

Wunjo/Vin ᚹ is the Rune of honors, rewards, respect, and strength. The warrior gains these as a result of fulfilling his duties to his people. These duties require great feats and sacrifices from the warrior. In many cases, only a few can accomplish them and they should be honored and recognized for their accomplishments.

The story of Earl Sigurd and the Raven Banner convey these elements. In this case, as with many battles fought by our Celtic ancestors, magick was involved.

Earl Sigurd, also known as Sigurd the Stout was a powerful man, defending his territories in Caithness against the Scots. He was renowned for his summertime expeditions plundering the Hebrides, western Scotland and Ireland.

Within the lore of Orkney his prowess is no less. The tales surrounding Sigurd abound with sorcery, miracles and omens. In these stories he is a magical, semi-mythical figure who fights with the power of the Old Gods at his side - the last great heathen Earl of Orkney.

One summer it happened that a Scottish earl called Finnleik challenged Sigurd to fight him on a particular day at Skitten. Sigurd's mother was a sorceress so he went to consult her, telling her that the odds against him were heavy, at least seven to one.

"Had I thought you might live for ever," she said, "I'd have reared you in my wool-basket. But lifetimes are shaped by what will be, not by where you are. Now, take this banner. I've made it for you with all the skill I have, and my belief is this: that it will bring victory to the man it's carried before, but death to the one who carries it."

It was a finely made banner, very cleverly embroidered with the figure of a raven, and when the banner fluttered in the breeze, the raven seemed to be flying ahead. Earl Sigurd lost his temper at his mother's words.

He got the support of the Orkney farmers by giving them back their land-right and then set out for Skitten to confront Earl Finnleik. The two sides formed up, but the moment they clashed Sigurd's standard-bearer was struck dead. The Earl told another man to pick up the banner but before long he'd been killed too. The Earl lost three standard bearers, but he won the battle and the farmers of Orkney got back their land-rights.

According to the Orkneyinga Saga, five years after the Battle of Svoldr - in which King Olaf Trygvasson perished - Earl Sigurd left Orkney for the last time, sailing for Ireland with the intention of supporting King Sigtrygg Silk-Beard, the King of Dublin.

In Ireland at the time an internal war was being waged between the King of Leinster and King Brian Boru. These opposing sides were seeking allies - so King Sigtrygg, and an alliance of Norsemen, fought with the King of Leinster.

The two sides met on Good Friday, 1014, and Sigurd's Raven Banner was unfurled. The ensuing battle was so fierce that it is said that in places the trees wept blood and the nearby River Tolka turned red.

Within Sigurd's ranks standard bearer after standard bearer fell.... Then Earl Sigurd called on Thorstein the son of Hall of the Side, to bear the banner, and Thorstein was just about to lift the banner, but then Asmund the White said, "Don't bear the banner! For all they who bear it get their death."

"Hrafn the Red!" called out Earl Sigurd, "bear thou the banner."

"Bear thine own devil thyself," answered Hrafn.

Then the earl said, "'Tis fittest that the beggar should bear the bag;'" and with that he took the banner from the staff and put it under his cloak."

From the moment he touched the standard his fate was sealed. As bearer he was sure to die - and he did, impaled shortly afterwards on an enemy's spear.

Back in Orkney there was a man called Hareck who had been ordered by the Earl to stay behind. Hareck reluctantly obeyed but only on the condition that he'd be the first to hear Sigurd's news upon his return.

On the evening of the Battle of Clontarf Hareck saw Sigurd riding home at the head of his warriors. Overjoyed at the return of the Earl, Hareck rode out to greet the returning heroes.
They were seen to meet but then the earth opened and the spectral horde rode under the hill. The hillside closed and Hareck was seen no more.

Nauthiz/Nauð ᚾ is the Rune of endurance and survival, fearlessness in the face of death, and the warriors will to carry on in the darkest of times. Attributes a warrior needs to accomplish his tasking, many times an impossible one. The great warriors are successful no matter the odds. They have been taught that "death is no excuse for failure." Failure is a word they have removed from their speech and mind, replacing it with solutions. The irony is realized by the warrior when the ONLY way to success is the sacrifice of his life. Without hesitation he offers his life in the final service and success of his people. In doing so, he has kept the honor and tradition of having no excuse for failure, not even death.

Boudica was the queen of the British Iceni tribe who led an uprising against the occupying forces of the Roman Empire. She was born around AD 25 to a royal family in Celtic Britain, and as a young woman she married Prasutagus, who later became king of the Iceni tribe. Her name meant victory.

Boudica's people once welcomed the Romans. Nearly 100 years earlier, when Gaius Julius Caesar made the first Roman foray into Britannia in 55 and 54 BC, the Iceni were among six tribes that offered him their allegiance. But this greatest of all Roman generals was unable to cope with either the power of the coastal tides or the guerrilla tactics of the other Britons who fought him. After negotiating a pro forma surrender and payment of tribute, Caesar departed.

For the next 97 years, no Roman military force set foot on British soil. The Iceni watched as their southern neighbors, the Catuvellauni, grew rich from exporting grain, cattle and hides, iron and precious metals, slaves and hunting dogs to Rome. From

Rome, they imported luxury goods such as wine and olive oil, fine Italian pottery, and silver and bronze drinking cups, and they minted huge numbers of gold coins at their capital, Camulodunum.

A century of Roman emperors came and went. Then, in 41 AD, Claudius (Tiberius Claudius Nero Germanicus) rose to the imperial purple. There were many practical reasons why he might have thought it useful to add Britannia to the empire, one being that the island was an important source of grain and other supplies needed in quantity by the Roman army. Stories abounded about the mineral wealth there. Outbreaks of unrest in Gaul were stirred up, so the Romans believed, by druid agitators from Britannia.

The Icenian king Prasutagus, celebrated for his long prosperity, had named the emperor his heir, together with his two daughters; an act of deference which he thought would place his kingdom and household beyond the risk of injury. The result was contrary, so much so that his kingdom was pillaged by centurions, his household by slaves; as though they had been prizes of war.

After Prasutagus died, the Roman procurator, Decianus Catus, arrived at the Iceni court with his staff and a military guard. He proceeded to take inventory of the estate. He regarded this as Roman property and planned to allocate a generous share for himself, following the habit of most Roman procurators. When Boudica objected, he had her flogged, her daughters raped, and the estates of the leading Iceni men were confiscated.

Boudica decided the Romans had ruled in Britannia long enough. The building fury of other tribes, such as the Trinovantes to the south, made them eager recruits to her cause. Despite the Roman ban, they had secretly stockpiled weapons. They armed themselves and planned their assault.

Boudica is described as very tall and grim in appearance, with a piercing gaze and a harsh voice. She had a mass of very fair hair which she grew down to her hips. She wore a great gold torque and a multi-colored tunic over which, was a thick cloak fastened with a brooch. Boudica's tunic, cloak and brooch were typical

Celtic dress for the time. The torque, the characteristic ornament of the Celtic warrior chieftain, was a metal band, usually of twisted strands of gold that fit closely about the neck, finished in decorative knobs worn at the front of the throat. Such torques symbolized a warrior's readiness to sacrifice his life for the good of his tribe. It is significant that Boudica wore one; they were not normally worn by women.

Boudica moved first against Camulodunum. Before she attacked, rebels inside the colonia conspired to unnerve the superstitious Romans. For no visible reason, the statue of Victory at Camulodunum fell down with its back turned as though it were fleeing the enemy. Delirious women chanted of destruction at hand. They cried that in the local senate-house outlandish yells had been heard; the theater had echoed with shrieks; at the mouth of the Thames a phantom settlement had been seen in ruins. A blood-red color in the sea and shapes like human corpses left by the ebb tide were interpreted hopefully by the Britons and with terror by the settlers.

Camulodunum pleaded for military assistance from Catus Decianus in Londinium, but he sent only 200 inadequately armed men to reinforce the town's small garrison. In their overconfidence, the Romans had built no wall around Camulodunum. In fact, they had leveled the turf banks around the

Legionary fortress and built on the leveled areas. Misled by the rebel saboteurs, they did not bother to erect ramparts, dig trenches or even evacuate the women and elderly.

Boudica's army overran the town, and the Roman garrison retreated to the unfinished temple, which had been one of the prime causes of the rebellion. After two days of fighting, it fell. Recent archaeological work shows how thorough the Britons were in their destruction. The buildings in Camulodunum had been made from a framework of timber posts encased in clay and would not have caught fire easily. But they were burned and smashed from one end of town to the other. So hot were the flames, some of the clay walls were fired as though in a pottery kiln and are preserved in that form to the present day.

The only Legionary force immediately available to put down the rebellion was a detachment of Legio IX Hispania, under the command of Quintus Petilius Cerialis Caesius Rufus, consisting of some 2,000 Legionaries and 500 auxiliary cavalry. Cerialis did not wait to gather a larger force, but set out immediately for Camulodunum. He never got there. Boudica ambushed and slaughtered his infantry. Cerialis escaped with his cavalry and took shelter in his camp at Lindum.

Suetonius, mopping up the operation on Mona, now learned of the revolt and set sail down the River Dee ahead of his army. He reached Londinium before Boudica, but what he found gave no cause for optimism. Like Camulodunum, Londinium was unwalled. About 15 years old, it had been built on undeveloped ground near the Thames River, by means of which supplies and personnel could be shipped to and from Rome. It was a sprawling town, with few large buildings that might be pressed into service as defensive positions — a smattering of government offices, warehouses and the homes of wealthy merchants. Catus Decianus had already fled to Gaul. Suetonius decided to sacrifice Londinium to save the province and ordered the town evacuated. Many of the women and elderly stayed, along with others who were attached to the place.

Boudica killed everyone she found when she reached Londinium. Dio described the savagery of her army: They hung up naked the noblest and most distinguished women and then cut off their breasts and sewed them to their mouths, in order to make the victims appear to be eating them; afterwards they impaled the women on sharp skewers run lengthwise through the entire body.

Verulamium, the old capital of the Catuvellauni tribe lying northwest of Londinium (outside of present-day St. Albans), met a similar fate. Rome had granted it the status of municipium, giving the townsfolk a degree of self-government and making its magistrates eligible for Roman citizenship. Boudica evidently punished the town for its close and willing association with Rome.

An estimated 70,000–80,000 Romans and British were killed in the three cities by those led by Boudica. Suetonius, meanwhile, regrouped his forces in the West Midlands, and despite being heavily outnumbered defeated the Britons in the Battle of Watling Street.

The crisis caused the Emperor Nero to consider withdrawing all Roman forces from Britain, but Suetonius' eventual victory over Boudica confirmed Roman control of the province. Boudica then either killed herself, so she would not be captured, or fell ill and died.

Algiz/Eolh ᛉ is the Rune of protection. The warrior lives to protect his people and project the will of the people. This is accomplished through the strength, cunning, training, and weapons of the warrior. The Rune's shape of a person with outstretched arms is suggestive of warding off an attack or threat. The warrior's charge is to protect the people.

Algiz/Eolh is associated with the Yew tree. Wood from the Yew tree was favored for long bows and spears. Death was delivered swiftly from the bow of deadly wood.

The Yew is also associated with death and rebirth. Yews were planted in sacred groves and locations. As the Christians invaded our ancestor's land, the sacred groves and locations were either destroyed or built over with churches. Many ancient Yews can still be found on church grounds and in graveyards. All parts of the Yew are toxic. They protect the ancient secrets of our ancestors with their deadly toxins.

Sowilo/Sól ᛋ is the Rune of victory, final triumph, and invincibility. It strengthens the warrior's will and soul. Like the lightening bolt, the warrior strikes hard and swift, obliterating the enemy.

Andraste is a warrior goddess, the goddess of victory, of ravens and of battles, similar in many ways to the Irish war goddess Morrigan. Her name means "the invincible one" or "she who has not fallen". Her presence was evoked on the eve of battle to curry favor. As a Goddess of divination, she was called upon to divine the outcome of battles and war. Andraste was venerated in woodland groves throughout Southern Britain. Her symbol is the hare.

As Andred, her Romanized name is Andraste, she was a lunar mother-goddess figure associated with fertility and love. In her dark aspect however, she was associated principally with warfare and specifically with victory. She is sometimes compared to the goddess Andarte, a deity worshipped by the Vocontii of Gaul.

The Iceni Queen Boudica, leader of a rebellion against the Roman occupation, propitiated Andraste in her campaigns against the Romans. Boudica released a hare as part of the rite of propitiation. It was a taboo in Britain to hunt hares, for fear that killing one might afflict the hunter with cowardice. Boudica released the animal hoping that the Romans might strike at it, and lose their courage.

The army of Queen Boudica sacked the cities of Camulodunum (Clochester), Londinium, (London) and Verlanium (St Albans). The sacking of London was exceptionally savage; the Roman women were rounded up and taken to a grove that was dedicated to the worship of the Celtic war goddess, Andraste. They were sacrificed, had their breasts cut off and stuffed into their mouths, and impaled with large skewers. This sacred grove was known to the Britons as Andraste's Grove, and was thought to have been somewhere in Epping Forest.

Boudica occupied a dual position both as tribal leader and as the manifestation of a Celtic Goddess. There is the mystery of Boudica's name; Boudica means 'victory'. She has been identified with Brigantia, the war goddess of the Brigantes. The Romans called Brigantia 'Victory' and even by 200AD altars were still being erected to her. She is linked with Morrigan, known as the Great Queen in Ireland. She is also associated with the triple war goddess whose three persons are Badb, Catha (Battle Raven), and Macha (Crow), whose sacred birds fed on the stake impaled heads of those slaughtered in battle. Boudica sacrificed those she defeated in battle to Andraste and she took no captives.

Mannaz/Maður ᛘ is the Rune of logic, memory, and intellect. It helps the warrior to gain a deeper understanding of himself. This is essential in the warrior's quest of self mastery and discipline.

Am fear a thug buaidh air fhein, thug e buaidh air namhaid

He who conquers himself, conquers an enemy

Gaelic Proverb

If you know the enemy and know yourself, you need not fear the result of a hundred battles. If you know yourself but not the enemy, for every victory gained you will also suffer a defeat. If you know neither the enemy nor yourself, you will succumb in every battle.

Sun Tzu – The Art of War

A Celtic warrior spent their entire life training and learning. Not just with physical feats and weapons, but they were expected to be versed in the laws, history, heritage, philosophy, politics, art, herbs, medicine, logistics, battle strategies, leadership, nature, agriculture, and many other subjects. The true warrior is not just a mindless minion that uses a weapon to destroy his enemy. All things are connected. The warrior is given the task to take the life energy of an enemy or offer his in exchange for the accomplishment of his tasking and his people.

Everything flows, out and in; everything has its tides; all things rise and fall; the pendulum-swing manifests in everything; the measure of the swing to the right is the measure of the swing to the left; rhythm compensates.

The Kybalion

Othala/Óðal ᛟ is the Rune of ancestral gifts (physical and otherwise), knowledge, and powers from past lives conveyed upon the warrior from himself and other family members. These are contained and conveyed through ancestral lines, which are integrated into the larger group of a common society such as a clan or country. The ancestral gifts, knowledge, and power can be shared and combined through marital unions or allegiances with other groups. The warrior helps to protect these gifts from misuse within the ancestral group and outsiders that would seize them, causing them to be lost to future generations. Protection, preservation, and the advancement of his family and country are the main motivators of the service offered by the warrior.

Chapter 9
Runes

Our ancestors were given sacred, magickal gifts and knowledge from the creators and their ancestors. These gifts and knowledge were passed from generation to generation as part of the ancestral inheritance. They were available to all, but resonated stronger with a few that could discern and understand their deeper meanings. The puppet masters desire to possess all magickal power and knowledge in their pursuit to control the masses. They bestow these powers and knowledge upon a select few who bartered their allegiances and services in exchange for what the puppet masters offer.

After decades of the forceful incursion of Christianity upon our ancestors, the ancestral knowledge and gifts were polluted, abolished, and replaced with the placebos of the church. There were a few that protected the ancestral knowledge and gifts through obscurity and secrecy. They preserved them for a time when their descendents would return, burning through the veil of forgetfulness to reclaim them. Using the Rune Perthro/Perð ᛕ the secrets of the Runes can be unlocked. Only those with the true intent to honor the Runes and those that gave them to us will be able to unlock the secrets and their powers.

The Elder Futhark and Armanen Runes are examined in this chapter. In addition, an article by Allan Webber, "The Runic Sky" is also presented.

Everything is hard before it is easy

Johann Wolfgang von Goethe

Allen Hartley

The Runes

The **Elder Futhark** (or **Elder Fuþark, Older Futhark, Old Futhark**) is the oldest form of the runic alphabet used by Germanic tribes for the Northwest Germanic and Migration period. Germanic dialects of the 2nd to 8th centuries for inscriptions are found on artifacts such as jewelry, amulets, tools, weapons and rune stones. In Scandinavia, the script was simplified to the Younger Futhark from the late 8th century, while the Anglo-Saxons and Frisians extended the Futhark which eventually became the Anglo-Saxon futhorc after Proto-English /a/ developed to /o/ in nasal environments.

Unlike the Younger Futhark, which remained in use until modern times, the knowledge of how to read the Elder Futhark was forgotten. It was not until 1865 that the Norwegian scholar Sophus Bugge managed to decipher it.

The Elder Futhark (named after the initial phoneme of the first six rune names: **F, U, Th, A, R and K**) consists of twenty-four runes, often arranged in three groups or ætts of eight each.

The word **"Rune"** is derived from **"Run"** (pronounced roon), an Anglo-Saxon word meaning **"Secret"** or **"Mystery"**. In contrast, the **"Futhark"** Alphabet is merely a means of conveying **letters** and **sounds**.

The Latin word **"Runa"** translates as **"Dart"**, which is descriptive of the Rune writing style, adapted from the Greek, to suit carving.

FEHU
Germanic: Fe (Fehu)
Gothic: Faihu
Norse: Fé
Anglo-Saxon: Feo, Feoh
Icelandic: Fé
Norwegian: Fe

This rune begins the Futhark alphabet and is the first of the three ættir. Characterizes the beast of burden. Slavish, stupid, slow, domesticated and mild. Cowardly. This is the sending rune used in magick. To grow, to wander, and to destroy.

White magick: Wealth, possessions, honors, property, money, and expansion. Power over one's environment, increase in wealth; fertility, mobility.

Black Magick: Instills cowardliness, dullness, breaks the spirit, binds an enemy; instills fear and dependence in an enemy.

ÜRUZ
Anglo-Saxon: UR
Norse: Úr
Icelandic: Úr
Norwegian: Ur
Germanic: Uraz (Uruz)
Gothic: Urus

Aurochs were a species of wild ox that lived in the European forests. By the 1600's it was hunted to extinction. This rune is the cosmic seed, beginnings and origins. It is masculine in nature and gives strength, endurance and athleticism. It is a rune of courage and boldness, freedom and rebellion. Ur represents the horn or the erect phallus, resurrection, life after death. Coming, being and passing away.

White Magick: Incites action, sexual potency. Freedom.

Black Magick: Used to threaten and destroy.

Magick: transfer of energies, used for projecting or drawing in of energy. Repeated use of the rune will gradually increase the amounts of energy one can handle at any given time. Helps in the growth of one's own reserves of power. Green and shimmering gold work well with the energies of this rune.

THURISAZ (Thorn)
Germanic: Thyth (Thurisaz)
Gothic: Thauris
Norse: Þurs
Anglo-Saxon: þorn
Icelandic: Þurs
Norwegian: Thurs

Rune of cutting, sharpness, and pain. Brute strength, destructive power of chaos and ruin. Also of death and regeneration, transformation and breaking down barriers. The power of this rune is wild and a strong mind/will is needed to direct it. Ur assists the energy of other runes it is used with to manifest in reality. Like a lightning bolt, Thorn brings on the energies of the berserker, energies this wild should only be used in war or attack.

Can raise and guide thunderstorms and direct lightning. The bloodstone has been used with this rune in the raising of thunderstorms. Hematite used with this rune can shield against electro-magnetic energies and is therefore helpful in deflecting curses.

In many German fairy tales such as "Sleeping Beauty" the prick of a thorn, pin or spindle casts a spell upon the victim.

Using this rune with a pointed crystal focuses energies and projects them.

Black Magick: Brings destruction and confusion. Thorn is used in the destruction of enemies and in curses. Used to control another or render the individual defenseless.

White Magick: Rune of healing. Enhances wisdom, courage, physical strength, independence and leadership.

ANSUZ (God)
Germanic: Aza (Ansuz)
Gothic: Ansus
Norse: Óss, Áss
Anglo-Saxon: Aesc, (Os, Ac)
Icelandic: Óss, Áss
Norwegian: As

Rune of the power of speech, destroys tyranny; "Your spiritual force sets you free". Order, the opposite of chaos, creative inspiration, magickal oratory ability and to persuade others and audiences through speech. Opens channels of self-expression and overcomes obstacles of every kind. Used to remove bindings. Assists in enhancing one's psychic and magickal abilities. Also used for work in invocation.

RAIDHO (Riding, travel)
Germanic: Reda (Raidho)
Gothic: Raida
Norse: Reið, Reiðr
Anglo-Saxon: Rad
Icelandic: Reið
Norwegian: Reid, Reidr

Rune of travel, journeys, and physical endurance. This rune has been used as a charm for travelers, this includes astral travel as well and Reidh acts as a guide for the dead in their journey in the underworld. Reidh also assists in astral travel.

This is also a rune of relocation such as moving house. Reidh also means seeking and striving; a quest and stepping into the unknown.

Magickally this rune when the energies are directed at another will make him/her restless and dissatisfied.

It creates changes in the life for good or ill depending on the other runes used in the working.

Reidh is a solar rune as it also symbolizes the chariot of Amon Ra, the Egyptian Sun God and represents the eightfold cycle of the Greater Sabbats. A rune of rhythm and music, Reidh makes one aware of the natural rhythms in life and helps one to better organize their time.

This rune represents justice and the essence of the law, while Tyr is the letter of the law.

KENAZ (Torch)
Germanic: Chozma (Kenaz)
Gothic: Kaun
Norse: Kaun
Anglo-Saxon: Cen, Ken
Icelandic: Kaun
Norwegian: Kaun

Rune of light. The light of the soul; also intellect.

The traveler on the road to the underworld carried Kaun to illuminate and guide.

The shape of this rune is of a delta for smooth flight and also penetrating. Magically this rune can be used for intellect, penetrating things as it carries energy. It also increases awareness and gives insight.

In black magick, it is used to incite stupidity and works so that the victim will remain unaware. This rune also represents sores, inflammations, swelling and boils.

Used for the control and harnessing of sexual energies and in working sex magick, often used with other fire runes and used to release the spirit into the realms of power.

This rune can be used to direct and influence the emotions of others. Bestows charisma, which is connected to the sexual energies. Useful in raising the kundalini. Fire agate and fire opal can be used with this rune, especially when working sex magick.

GEBO (Gift)
Germanic: Geuua (Gebo)
Gothic: Giba
Norse: Gipt, Giöf
Anglo-Saxon: Geofu (Gyfu)
Icelandic: Gjöf
Norwegian: Giof

This is a rune of sacrifice and giving. Something of personal value given freely. This is a rune of initiation where we make personal sacrifices to obtain knowledge, power and wisdom.

Magickally, Gipt is a bringer of gifts. Gipt relates to weddings and alliances. Gipt is also used in sex magick and binding spells. Can be used to bind another to an unwanted obligation and can be used in casting love spells.

When used in Black Magick, it brings pain and sacrifice upon the victim with no reward. Used with the Isa rune, the combination is powerful in binding enemies.

Emerald and jade are the gems used with this rune.

WUNJO
Germanic: Uuinne (Wunjo)
Gothic: Winja
Norse: Vend
Anglo-Saxon: Wynn
Icelandic: Vin
Norwegian: Wynn

Wunjo is a rune of honors and rewards. Our efforts are rewarded.

Vend is bliss merging with light. This rune is excellent for banishing depression. Good for raising confidence and self-esteem.

Helps to unite family members and mend friendships. Breaks down barriers between one's self and others.

Authority, respect and strength.

When directed for black magick, this rune can be used to instill overconfidence and trust of the wrong things in others, leading to their downfall.

Vend is also a rune of healing as it binds the healing of the mind with the healing of the physical self. Wards off diseases. Good for working with the heart chakra. Topaz enhances this rune as well as rose quartz.

HAGL (Hail)
Germanic: Haal (Hagalaz)
Gothic Hagl
Norse: Hagall
Anglo-Saxon: Hægl
Icelandic: Hagall
Norwegian: Hagall, Hagl

This rune represents hailstones. Involuntary sacrifice with no reward; a rune of suffering and injustice. A rune of destruction, disaster and violence.

This rune is mainly used in black magick sending destruction in the form of whatever runes are used with it, delivering violent loss and pain.

Hagl is a rune of completion and the number nine. Nine is the greatest German number of power, as it equals the number of the main chakras.

NAUTHIZ (Need)
Germanic: Noicz (Nauthiz)
Gothic: Nauths
Norse: Nauð, Nauðr
Anglo-Saxon: Nied (Nyd)
Icelandic: Nauð
Norwegian: Naudr, Naud

Nauthiz is a rune of endurance and will. The mental strength to last. It represents the dark night of the soul. It is connected to the Hagl rune.

When used in white magick, this rune gives defiance and the strength to carry on when all hope seems lost. It is a rune of survival and fearlessness in the face of death. When directed at another, this rune can give the spiritual strength to carry on and endure in the face of disaster. Develops the will and self-sufficiency. The rune of trial and testing.

Used in black magick, it brings suffering and hardship. Nauthiz is a rune of friction and resistance. A rune of banishings and cleansing by fire.

Nauthiz can be used in counter-spells.

Obsidian is the gem used with this rune. Obsidian is also the gem of the planet Saturn, which bestows hardship and endurance.

ISA (Ice)
Germanic: Icz (Isa)
Gothic Eis
Norse: Íss
Anglo-Saxon: Is
Icelandic: Íss
Norwegian: Is

Isa is a rune of binding. Used with other runes, it acts to bind and shield the energies and keep them from interacting with each other.

It represents stealth and sneakiness and is used in operations where one wishes to proceed undetected; Iss bestows invisibility. In nature, ice creeps up on the land, quietly freezing and immobilizing everything in its path. The unaware fall victim to it.

Magickally, Iss is a rune of binding and preventing action through hidden means. It can halt a plan and prevent something from developing. It is used to conceal and can render a victim unaware of impending personal disaster to where any actions attempted will be too late in coming. It is also used in preventing any action and can ruin planned activity.

Isa freezes action and is the rune of cold, barren stillness and death. Isa is the exact opposite of Fehu. As Fehu is a rune of movement, Isa is a rune of binding.

Used in ritual against another, it brings barrenness, prevents prosperity, causes depression, and serves as an obstacle to action.

Can be used to cause paralyzing fear or obsession and to prevent or stop movement, both that of growth and disintegration. Often used in revenge spells and defense, it helps focus the will of the operator.

On a more positive note, this rune is helpful in void meditation, as it acts to still and also helpful in concentration, bringing calmness and guidance. Care needs to be taken as the rune can also make the user dull and/or obsessive.

Isa works to calm hysteria, hyperactivity and restlessness.

JERA (Year)
Germanic: Gaar (Jera)
Gothic: Jer
Norse: Ár
Anglo-Saxon: Ger (Jara)
Icelandic: Ár
Norwegian: Jara, Ar

Jera is a rune of cycles and is symbolic of the harvest where the efforts of planting and work in the fields are rewarded with crops. Ingwaz is the seed planted, Berkano is the earth that receives it and Jera is the growth and the harvest.

Ar represents the cycles of change. Life cycles, lunar cycles, the cycles of the seasons and changes. Ar is in contrast to Íss where everything stops. It signifies the return of the Sun and brings action. Ar symbolizes a vortex of cycling energy; the eight-fold wheel of life, the point inside of the circle, which is the glyph for the Sun meaning regeneration.

Ár is the rune of patience and awareness, moving in harmony with natural cycles. This rune is excellent for working with nature and is a rune of fruitfulness.

A rune of long term planning and persistence and ensures the success of plans.

When used in magickal operations, it can bring a reversal of personal fortunes. Like the Tarot Card, the Wheel of Fortune, Ar can reverse circumstances so misfortune is replaced with luck and visa-versa.

When used in black magick, this rune can bring the worst possible aspects of an individual's Wyrd to manifest and develops the forces of self-destruction.

The stone is moss agate.

EIHWAZ
Germanic: Ezck (Eihwaz)
Gothic: Eiws
Anglo-Saxon: Yr (Eoh)
Norwegian: (Eo)

Used in necromancy (communicating with the dead). It is a rune of death and power over the dead. Eihwaz strengthens the will and can be used in past life regressions to gain knowledge and wisdom from prior lives.

It represents the kundalini force. This rune shields the soul through all kinds of hardship. Like the planet Pluto, it is a rune of transformation through death and rebirth and rules over deep and powerful transformation on all levels.

Smoky quartz is used with this rune. Both can be used to activate and raise the kundalini.

PERTHRO
Germanic: Pertra (Perthro)
Gothic: Pairthra
Norse: Perð
Anglo-Saxon: Peordh (Pertra)
Icelandic: Perð, (Plástur)
Norwegian: (Pertra)

Perthro is a rune used in divination. Through this rune, one can gain the knowledge and wisdom of other runes. This rune acts as protection against the destructive forces of certain runes. Through Perthro, we can intuitively discover lost knowledge of all of the runes. Perthro is the rune of meditation. Onyx is the stone used with this rune.

ALGIZ
Germanic: Algis, Algiz or Elhaz
Gothic: Algs
Anglo-Saxon: Eolh
Norwegian: Elgr

This rune is used for protection. It is also used in consecration and the banishing of negative energies. It is excellent for the operator to wear when performing dangerous rituals as it protects against negative energies.

Black tourmaline is the stone used with this rune.

SOWILO
Germanic: Sugil (Sowilo)
Gothic: Sauil
Norse: Sól
Anglo-Saxon: Sigel
Icelandic: Sól
Norwegian: Sol
Old Danish: Sulu
Old German: Sil, Sigo, Sulhil

Sowilo is the rune of the Sun and can be used in masculine magick. Sowilo is a rune of invincibility, and final triumph. This rune is movement and action and bestows the will to take action.

Sowilo is used to strengthen the will and confidence. It enhances one's strength of spirit. Brings out one's leadership abilities and one's ability to inspire others.

Sowilo is used to understand the energy forces in the world and on the astral. When used with other runes, it activates and empowers them.

Sól symbolizes the chakras and the lightening bolt, spark of life. Kundalini is like lightening and flashes in the brain when it connects with the 6th chakra. It can be used in meditation and to empower the chakras.

It has both shielding and combative properties.

Diamond is the gem to use with Sól.

TIWAZ
Germanic: Tys (Tiwaz)
Gothic: Teiws
Norse: Týr
Anglo-Saxon: Tir, Tiw
Icelandic: Týr
Norwegian: Ty

Instills courage and honor. Tyr is the rune of justice. Used for stability and the binding of chaotic energies. Good for defense and revenge workings as it represents justice. Bloodstone and hematite are the stones used with this rune.

BJÖRK
Germanic: Bercna (Berkano)
Gothic: Bairkan
Norse: Bjarkan
Anglo-Saxon: Beroc
Icelandic: Bjarkan
Norwegian: Bjarkan

This rune can be used in workings for female fertility, feminine magick, and nurturing. It is used in concealment and protection. This rune symbolizes feminine energies. It is an old Pagan custom to enclose a child at birth with the protective energies of Berkano, which remain with him/her throughout his/her life.

EHWAZ
Germanic: Eys (Ehwaz)
Gothic: Aihwa
Norse: Ehol, Ior
Anglo-Saxon: Eoh
Icelandic: Eykur
Norwegian: Eh, Eol

Eykur represents the horse. It is also closely identified with Castor and Pollux the Gemini twins.

Eihwaz is used to see into the future and for psychic communication. Used in spiritual divination to understand the will of the Gods.

Like the fourth chakra, this rune unites opposites. This rune forges bonds and is used to seal marriages and friendships.

Eykur is used to empower thoughtforms and bring them under the control and will of the mage. Can be used to bind another's thoughts and actions to the operator's will.

When used with other runes, Eihwaz unites the energies harmoniously.

MANNAZ
Germanic: Manna (Mannaz)
Gothic: Manna
Norse: Maðr
Anglo-Saxon: Mann
Icelandic: Maður
Norwegian: Madr

Rune of logic and the left side of the brain. Used for enhancing intellect and strengthening the memory. Helps one to gain more knowledge of one's self, which is essential in working magick.

Amethyst is the Gem to use with Mannaz.

Lögur
Germanic: Laaz (Laguz)
Gothic: Lagus
Norse: Lögr
Anglo-Saxon: Lagu
Icelandic: Lögur
Norwegian: Laukr

Conceals and symbolizes the unknown. Reveals and counteracts poisons. The hidden is revealed. Assists in the awareness of energies and enhances one's sensitivity. Good for dowsers and pendulum workers. Helps in astral work. Can be used to enhance physical and psychic strength. Used in feminine magick and masking the forces of other runes.

INGWAZ
Norse: Ing, Ingvarr
Gothic: Iggws
Germanic: Enguz (Ingwaz)
Anglo-Saxon: Ing
Icelandic: Ing
Norwegian: Ing

INGWAZ is the male counterpart to Berkano. It represents the God "Ing." Ingwaz is the rune in which power is stored. Converts active power into potential power. Like a crystal, this rune stores energy until it is needed. It is a magickal reserve.

Can deprive a man of his masculinity or anyone, male or female of their life force.

Ivory is used with INGWAZ.

DAGAZ
Germanic: Daaz (Dagaz)
Gothic: Dags
Norse: Dagr
Anglo-Saxon: Daeg
Icelandic: Dagur
Norwegian: Dagr

Represents the climax of orgasm where the objective of the working is realized. Like the planet Uranus, this rune gives flashes of intuition and knowledge.

Useful in raising the kundalini.

Best if used with other runes that enhance wisdom and awareness.

ÖDHAL
Germanic: Utal (Othala)
Gothic: Othal
Norse: Oðal
Anglo-Saxon: Otael (Ethel)
Icelandic: Óðal
Norwegian: Ödal

Óðal is the rune of property and land, ancestry and heritage. Used to tap into one's racial memory for ancestral knowledge.

Unlike Fehu, this rune represents property that is rooted and not mobile, a putting down of roots.

Óðal be used to incite racism and cultural prejudices.

Othala represents the circle/sphere; the boundary.

Petrified wood works well with Othala; brings out memories of past lives, talents and wisdom of previous incarnations.

The Armanen Runes

The 18 "Armanen Runes", also known as the "Armanen Futharkh" came to Guido von List while in an 11-month state of temporary blindness after a cataract operation on both eyes in 1902. This vision in 1902 opened what List referred to as his "inner eye", via which the "Secret of the Runes" was revealed to him. List stated that his Armanen Futharkh were encrypted in the Hávamál (Poetic Edda), specifically in stanzas 138 to 165, with stanzas 146 through 164 reported as being the 'song' of the 18 runes.

The Armanen runes are still used today by some Ásatrú adherents who consider the Armanen runes to have religious and/or divinatory value.

List's system was based on the structure of a Hexagonal Crystal. You can shine light through a crystal at different angles and project all 18 of the Armanen runes.

List's rune row was rather rigid; while the runes of the past had had sharp angles for easy carving, his were to be carefully and perfectly made so that their shape would be a reflection of the 'frozen light', a pattern that he had found in his runes. All of his runes could be projected by shining the light through a hexagonal crystal under certain angles. Rune Hagal is the 'mother-rune' because its shape represents that of a hexagonal crystal.

Karl Hans Welz states that the "crystalline structure of quartz is the "hexagonal system" which is also one of the bases of the Runic symbolism (the hexagon with the three inscribed diameters)." and that "The hexagonal cross section of quartz and the fact that all of the 18 Sacred Futhork Runes are derived from the geometry of the hexagon is the basis of an enormous increase in crystal

FA (f,v)

Exoteric meaning: Changes, new beginnings, growth, change of residence, travel, animals, mobile possessions, fire.

Esoteric meaning: Original fire, to destroy and shred, creative father principle, guidance, Father-God principle.

Fa is the Rune of original fire. It is a Rune that symbolizes the cosmos and the universe. FA symbolizes fire that acts creatively. It is will that sparks manifestation down to the material levels. FA is one of the Runes that rules the Salamanders, spirits of the fire element. It symbolizes change from within the creative levels and spiritual creation. FA represents the Phoenix that rises from its ashes. It is a Rune of fate, of mobility, and of wealth.

Fa is used to attract and absorb Solar and Lunar energy as well as the energies of the planets and fixed stars. It is used to transfer energies.

The first promises to help helpfully in the struggle and in misery and in every difficulty.

The root word Fa, which is symbolized as the primordial word in this rune, is the conceptual foundation of arising, being (doing, working, ruling), and of passing away to new arising -- and so of the transitoriness of all existence and therefore of the stability of the ego in constant transformation. This rune conceals, therefore, the skaldic solace that true wisdom only lives for the evolution of the future, while only the fool mourns over decay: Generate your luck and you will have it!

Time of the Year: December 22 through January 12

Number: 1

UR (u,w)

Exoteric meaning: That which is permanent, that which lasts, good fortune, money, physician, medical help, healing powers, aurochs, resurrection, life after death.

Esoteric meaning: Original cause, origin, root of all material and cosmic phenomena, contact with the transcendent, contact with the dead, life after physical death, Mother-God, Creative Mother Principle. The primordial, eternity, primal fire, primal light, primal bull, primal generation,

UR is the Rune of original cause of cosmic and planetary events. It is the Rune of original time. It is time at the threshold of creation: time-less time where space-time is irrelevant. UR connects with cause of causes, with original creation, with original immortality, and with original law of vibration.

UR is the threshold of creation that Fa energizes with its impulse. It is creation for which created deities (or, even more ridiculous, anthropomorphic collective egregors of religions) take undeserved credit. It is original knowledge.

Mythological speaking the roots of the world tree, Yggdrasill, are in UR. It is here where the tree Norns, goddesses of fate and destiny, are spinning the threads of the web of time that determines the fates of humans and of gods. Here the fountain of wisdom is running to which the gods (think also of the gods within!) descend to gain knowledge and wisdom.

The basis of all manifestation is the Primeval. Whoever is able to recognize the cause of an event, to him the phenomenon itself does not seem to be an insoluble puzzle -- be this fortunate or unfortunate -- and therefore he is able to banish misfortune or increase luck, but also to recognize false evil and false luck as such. Therefore: Know yourself, then you will know all!

Time of the year: January 13 through February 3

Number: 2

THORN (th, d)

Exoteric meaning: **Will to act, setting of goal, power to become. Thorn.**

Esoteric meaning: **Return, new emergence from what's apparently old and dried-up, formative power of the seed. Thunder, thunderbolt, lightning flash.**

THORN is the Rune of activity and of the active mind. In this capacity, the Rune THORN is symbolized as the Rune of the master of the swords. It is a Rune of active exchange and one of the Runes that represent Thor's Hammer.

THORN is a Rune of polarities. While FA is the spark of creation, UR the chaos at the threshold of creation, THORN symbolizes the emerging of opposite polarities from the zero point energy of chaos. From the realm of opposite polarities THORN reaches much deeper into multiple polarities of an infinite order.

As Rune of opposing polarities THORN represents life and death, hot and cold, light and darkness, etc. It is a Rune of opposites that actually are polarities of one and the same process. Therefore THORN is also a rune of eternal return and as such contains in itself the mystery of the thorn that awakens from sleep.

The THORN that touches the zero energy of chaos brings forth continuous creation.

THORN is the Rune of the dowsing rod, of lightning and thunder, of magnetic transfer and of metal telepathy.

THORN awakens in us the will to act and to creatively act upon our universe. It helps us get in touch with the continuous change of day and night, waning and waxing, life and death. THORN protects us against attacks, especially magical attacks. The mantra of THORN strengthens the aura.

The thorn of death is that which Wotan put the disobedient Valkyrie, Brünnhilde, into a death sleep (compare Sleeping Beauty, and so on), but in contrast to this it is also the thorn of life (phallus), with which death is conquered by rebirth. This threatening sign surely dulls the opposing weapon of the one going to his death, as well as the force of the powers of death, through a constant renewal of life in rebirth. Therefore: Preserve your ego!

Time of the year: February 4 through 25

Number: 3

OS (o)

Exoteric meaning: **Speech, talk, discussion, successful as a speaker, mouth, breath that evolves, uterus**

Esoteric Meaning: **Idea of that which is given, idea of that which is evolving. Gods, mouth, arising, ash, ashes.**

OS is the Rune of the fourth element, which is the element of conscious manifestation. It is a Rune of Odic energy that frees us from the bondage of the perceived material world.

Being the Rune of conscious manifestation it can give us strong magical powers. OS teaches us to recognize the laws that govern the magical universe and the magical hyperspaces.

You can use OS to enhance the growth of your spiritual powers. You may use OS also to draw powerful astral and mental energies.

The mouth, the power of speech! Spiritual power working through speech (power of suggestion) bursts physical fetters and gives freedom, it itself conquers all conquerors, who only gain advantages through physical force, and it destroys all tyranny. (In the struggle for existence, the folk who always remain lasting winners are those who develop themselves with the preservation of their moral force. With the disappearance of morality, higher spiritual and intellectual rank is also lost, as history--the final judgment--will prove.) Therefore: Your spiritual force makes you free!

Allen Hartley

Time of the year: February 26 through March 20

Number: 4

RIT (r)

Exoteric meaning: Right, order, the judge, advice, salvation, and money.

Esoteric meaning: Original law, that which flows away, religious feeling, and ritual action. Cosmic law, rat, red, wheel, rod, right.

RITA = right. RIT is the Rune of original law, of Divine law. It connects with the powers of all-justice. RIT signifies religion, inner strength, and ritual. It is the Rune of the cosmic rhythm of the worlds. RIT symbolizes movement, rotation, wheels, and spiraling development and unfolding. It is the Rune of the rolling Sun-wheel, of rhythmic and of dance.

The thrice-hallowed Cosmic Law, the solar wheel, the primal fire itself! The exalted introspective awareness or subjectivity of the Aryans was their consciousness of their own godliness, for internity is just being with one's self, and to be with one's self is to be with the Nordic God. As long as a people possesses unspoiled their entire original internity as a natural people (the people as a natural people is not being in a savage condition, for uncivilized savages live in the bondage of the most horrible shamanism; the people as a natural people, on the contrary, stipulates a high level of culture, yet free from any kind of false sophistication), it also has no cause to worship an external divinity, for an external divine service bound by ceremony is only made obvious when one is not able to find the Nordic God in one's own innermost being, and begins to see this outside his ego and outside the world -- up there in the starry heaven. The less internal the person is, the more outward his life becomes. The more a people loses its internity, the more pompous and ceremonialised its outward manifestations become -- in the character of its government, law, and cult (all of which will begin to emerge as separate ideas). But they should remain one in the knowledge: What I believe is what I know, and so I also live it out. For this reason, the Aryan divine internity is also the basis for a proud disdain for death among the Aryans and for their limitless trust in the Nordic God and in the self, which expresses itself gloriously in the primal law of the Aryans and which has the fifth rune as its symbolic word sign. Therefore, this rune says: I am my right (rod), this right is indestructible, therefore I am myself indestructible, because I am my right.

Time of the year: March 21 through April 12.

Number: 5

KA (k, g, ch, q)

Exoteric meaning: Art, capability, artist, genius, being favored, procreation, the child, force, that which is established.

Esoteric meaning: Female principle in the universe, as executive power of balancing justice.

KA is a sexual Rune. It is the Rune of capability, the occultist, and of higher mysteries.

Like THORN, KA is a Rune of protection against magical attacks. KA gives intuition, inspiration, and it connects with the universe. KA connects with higher polarity. It increases courage.

The world tree Yggdrasill serves in the narrower sense as the Aryan tribal tree, beside which the tribal trees of foreign races are seen as foreign trees.

The runic concept haun, kunna (maid, for example, in the name Adelgunde) demonstrates the feminine principle in the All in a purely sexual sense. The tribe, the race, is to be purely preserved; it may not be defiled by the roots of the foreign tree. If it were nevertheless to happen, however, such would be of little use to the foreign trees, because its foreign scion would grow to become its raging foe. Therefore: Your blood, your highest possession.

Allen Hartley

Time of the year: April 13 through May 5.

Number: 6

HAGAL (h)

Exoteric meaning: That which cares and maintains, protects, and preserves; that which is motherly; wisdom, harmony, salvation, blessing, protects from hail and fire.

Esoteric meaning: Eternal change, caring and maintaining principal in the universe, Higher Self, God in us. All hedge, to enclose, hail, to destroy

Fire refers here to "the fire of thirst." HAG-ALL = take care of the universe. It contains the symbolism of the omnipresent and all-penetrating creative energy.

HAGAL is the symbolism of the builder-architect of the worlds. The seven is the rhythm of the Solar System. It connects with he BNE ELOHIM, Venus-entities (Venus = 7), who create the world in an eternal NOW. HAGAL is the Rune of the world tree, of the world, of the tree of life. It is a combination of MAN and YR, NOD and EH. HAGAL is maintenance and equilibrium of the moving universe. It is the Rune of the zodiac, and mother of all Runes that signifies continuous change. HAGAL leads to the spiritual leader. In the microcosm it represents man, in the macrocosm it represents the universe.

HAGAL gives protection and harmony. It serves as the solid point within the flight of phenomena. It eliminates the burning thirst for thing that are not important in life. It provides consciousness of Oneness with the Divine. It brings spiritual powers and wisdom. It increases the functions of the pineal gland and of the solar plexus.

Introspective awareness, the consciousness to bear his Nordic God with all his qualities within himself, produces a high self-confidence in the power of the personal spirit, which bestows magical power, a magical power, which dwells within all persons, and a power, which can persuade a strong spirit to believe in it without any doubt. Wotan was one of these rare persons. Borne by this consciousness which has no doubt inherent, the chosen one controls the physical and spiritual realms, which he contains comprehensively, and thereby he feels himself to be All Powerful. Therefore: Harbor the All in yourself, and you will control the All!

Time of the year: May 6 through May 28.

Number: 7

NOD (n)

Exoteric meaning: That which cannot be averted, separation, stress, karmic debt, karmic need, but with outlook for change of karma, banishing ill fortune by means of accepting karma and karmic law.

Esoteric meaning: The decision of the Norns, karma paid-for, and cause-effect relations. Capability to restructure karma. Need, Norn, Compulsion of fate.

NOD is the Rune of karma. In the Northern tradition, NOD is the Rune of the Norn, goddess of destiny. It is the Rune of karmic debts (the Norn SKULD), of karmic law, of karmic need. NOD signifies Divine justice that balances. "Hate" in the song refers to unresolved karma. Nod helps to master your karma after you have accepted it. NOD symbolizes the appearance out of the infinite, out of the undefined. It connects with the Divine that manifests itself within the finite universe, for "a god who does not manifest itself is dead" (Feuerbach).

NOD makes you aware of your karmic debts and it helps dissolve karma. It leads to truth and fitting into the cosmic order, or the Divine Plan. NOD brings the protection of high spiritual entities of our Solar System. Use your karma and live it consciously.

The need rune blooms on the nail of the Norn! This is not need (distress) in the modern sense of the word, but rather the compulsion of fate -- that the Norns fix according to primal laws. With this, the organic causality of all phenomena is to be understood. Whoever is able to grasp the primal cause of a phenomenon, and whoever gains knowledge of organically lawful evolution and the phenomena arising from it, is also able to judge their consequences just as they are beginning to ferment. Therefore, he commands knowledge of the future and also understands how to settle all strife through the constraint of the clearly recognized way of fate. Therefore: Use you your fate, do not strive against it!

Time of the year: May 29 through June 20.

Number: 8

IS (i)

Exoteric meaning: Positivity, activity, will, self-domination, influence, personal power, magical power, power to banish evil.

Esoteric meaning: Unity in the universe, duration, magical powers, and action in the cosmos. Ice and Iron.

Rune of the ego, of self-discipline, of discipline. Rune of the personality, of the magical powers of self-consciousness. Symbolizes will, action, power, and personality. The ego in the microcosm, the ONEness that connects everything created to ONE. The eternal Divine Love that transcends the lower ego. The Rune of completion. The unicorn, the magic wand, the number of the Moon.

IS strengthens the personality (ship) by calming emotionally charged thoughts (the wind on the billowing floods), controls thoughts. IS procures psychic powers through self-discipline and through elimination of that which is unnecessary. IS leads to Divine Magic.

Through the consciousness, which has no doubt inherent, of personal spiritual power the waves are bound -- made to freeze -- they stiffen as if ice. But not only the waves, all of life is obedient to the compelling will. Countless examples of the Agis shield (related to the Aegis hjálmer, the helm of awe or terror, part of the Nibelungen treasure won by Sigurdhr) of Wotan, such as the Gorgon's head of the Athenians, the Aegis helm, all the way down to the hunting lore and practice of causing an animal to freeze (the magic of making something freeze in hunting lore and practice is substantiated as hypnosis), and modern hypnosis, are all based on the hypnotic power of forceful will of the spirit symbolized by this ninth rune. Therefore: Win power over yourself and you will have power over everything in the spiritual and physical worlds that strives against you.

Time of the year: June 21 through July 14

Number: 9

AR (a)

Exoteric meaning: **All that, which is beautiful and Sun-like, change to good, primal fire, nobles, Aryans, virtues, honor, glory, rewarding work.**

Esoteric meaning: **Completion, light, Divine spirit, Sun.**

Rune of the Light, of the Sun. Wisdom, beauty, virtue, trust, honor, fame. Rune of the initiate. Symbolism of the solar child that returns home from darkness.

AR allows control of subconscious thought patterns and recognizes their point of origin, or roots (meditate on the stanza!). Rune of reframing. Brings change from within. Rune of certainty that dissolves doubts. AR attracts solar prana.

The Ar, the primal fire, the sun, the light, will destroy spiritual as well as physical darkness, doubt, and uncertainty. In the sign of the Ar the Aryans -- the sons of the sun -- founded their law, the primal law of the Aryans, of which the eagle (Aar) is the hieroglyph. It sacrifices itself, as it consecrates itself in a flaming death, in order to be reborn. For this reason it was called the fanisk (fan = generation, ask = arising, beginning; therefore: fanisk = the beginning of generation through rebirth; fanisk later became the phoenix, and thus is the phoenix explained; compare Wotan's rune song: I know that I hung on a wind cold tree) and later phoenix. Therefore it is read as a symbolic hieroglyph when an eagle is laid on the funeral pyre of a celebrated hero to indicate that the dead hero rejuvenatingly prepares himself in death for rebirth in order to strive for a still more glorious future life in human form in spite of all the restrictions of the powers of darkness -- all of which crumble before the Ar: Respect the primal fire!

Time of the year: July 15 through August 7.

Number: 10

SIG/SOL (s, z)

Exoteric meaning: Victory, success, gain, successful fight, achieved goal, school.

Esoteric meaning: Salvation by light, inspiration, and soul. Sun and column.

SIG is the Rune of the light, the Rune of the Sun, Rune of victory, success, and good luck. It is the Solar Light in spiritual contemplation. It symbolizes the path "from God to God," the path of the soul. Rune of the spiritual ray, of inspiration. SIG brings success, overcomes material limitations, and increases power of the spirit. It gives knowledge, wisdom, and illumination. It increases the power of visualization, and psychic powers.

Sal and Sig! -- salvation and victory (Heil und Sieg). This millennia old Aryan greeting and battle cry is also again found in a variant form in the widespread call of inspiration: alaf sal fena! (All solar salvation to him who is conscious of power, that is, able to reproduce!) This has become symbolized by the eleventh sign of the Futharkh as the sig rune (victory rune): The creative spirit must conquer!

Time of the year: August 8 through August 30.

Number: 11

TYR (t, d)

Exoteric meaning: Beginning, creation, excitation, power, success, wisdom, duties fulfilled, art of concealment and hiding.

Esoteric meaning: Rebirth into the light – life of the soul. Týr, the Sun God and Sword God; to generate, to turn, to conceal; thus Tarnkappe, the cap of concealment,

Rune of the god of swords. Rune of the god who sacrifices himself, certain of resurrection. Rune of initiation, of reincarnation, of being born again. Hammer of Thor. TYR helps overcome the material world, the fear of material death. Brings victory of spirit over matter. Recalling of past lives.

The reborn Wotan, that is, the renewed Wotan who has climbed down from the world tree after his self sacrifice, as well as the renewed fanisk (phoenix), which flies up out of the ashes, is personified in the young Sun God and Sword God, Týr.

According to the rule of mysticism, every magical belief moves parallel to mythology, in that the mythic pattern is adopted in analogies to human earthly processes, in order to reach results similar to those given in the myths. While esotericism on the basis of the well-known bifidic biune dyad recognizes the mystic one in the mystic many--and therein it sees the fate of the All and hence of every individual--in eternal change from passing away to rebirth. As Wotan returned after his self sacrifice--which is to be understood not merely as his death, but rather as his whole life--in a renewed body, so also does every single person return after every life in human form with a renewed body through a rebirth--which is equally a self sacrifice. For this reason, tar means to generate, to live, and to pass away--and therefore Týr is the reborn young sun.

So too is the twelfth rune at the same time a victory rune, and hence it is carved into sword blades and spearheads as a sign to give victory. It shall be said: "Fear not death--it cannot kill you!"

Time of the year: August 31 through September 22.

Number: 12

BAR (b, p)

Exoteric meaning: Becoming, birth, being projected, help in birth, son, bread, song, fountain, mountains.

Esoteric meaning: Meaning of life on this planet, in this world. Birth, song, folk song, folk, German, bier

Rune of revelation, Rune of birth of the spirit. Rune of birth, of spiritual rebirth. Return to the Mothers, to the empire of HEL. Life, hopes, wishes. Rune of continuous transformation, death and rebirth.

Development of higher spiritual, mystical and psychic capabilities. Lead to inner freedom and outer independence. Helps birth, spiritual birth.

In the bar rune the spiritual life in the All, the eternal life in which human life between birth and death means but one day, stands in contrast to this day in the life in human form, which goes from bar (birth) through bar (life as a song) to bar (bier, death. This (day in the) life is bounded by birth and death, and even if destiny has not at once appointed a sword death for the bairn--he is still exposed to this and many another danger.

For in spite of the determination and dispensation of destiny, dark chance, rules, based on the free will of men, and it is against such a maleficent degree of chance that the sacred blessing is supposed to work.

Actually there is no such thing as chance, for all events without exception are in the great web of fate--as warp and woof--all well ordered, but what concerns woof, the cross weave, is even for clairvoyants only visible with difficulty; the recognizable straight warp of the effects of earlier causes, effects that are always in turn other causes that trigger coming effects-- which again form causes that trigger effects, in an unending genetic series--is visible and calculable to seers and initiates; however, it is difficult to tell ahead of time the effects of the woof of the fate of other egos or whole groups of them, and to tell when they will touch, cross, or otherwise influence our woof of fate; these work on our woof of fate-- which is comparable to the woof in a fabric, like the woof or cross weave in such a fabric, and because these incalculable influences often suddenly and unexpectedly disturb our own woof of fate, these are called chance, without, however, having considered a chance occurrence as something irregular or lawless-- that cannot be! But perhaps as something incalculable; the oldest Aryan mystics already recognized this, and therefore portrayed the rulers of fate, the three Norns, as weavers of fate, who out of the warp and woof weave the raiment of time, that is, fate.

The Germanic people did not recognize any blind faith. They did believe in predestination in the greatest sense, but they intuitively saw that many restrictions (chance accidents!) stand in the way of the completion and fulfillment of predestination in order to fulfill and steal personal power. Without these accidents, for example, every pine tree would have to be strictly symmetrical in all its parts; one would have to be the same as the next, while in fact no two can be found that are exactly alike, and so too it would have to be in human life; all without difference, uniform and equal. Therefore: Your life stands in the hand of the Nordic God; trust it in you!

Time of the year: September 23 through October 15.

Number: 13

LAF (l)

Exoteric meaning: Life, experience, test, and temptations by life-circumstances, water, sea, and good management.

Esoteric meaning: Test of life. School of the lives. Relations. Primal law, life, downfall, defeat.

The ancients used the mythological method to talk of that, which is psychological, psychic, and spiritual. LAF is the Rune of life, of the law of life, of the original laws of the universe, of the original water. Rune of the sea. Rune of the etheric part of the body. Rune of initiation, which experience life on earth as a process of initiation. LAF brings understanding of the life processes, of true religion.

The intuitive knowledge of the organic essence of the All, and therefore of the laws of nature, forms the unshakable foundation of Aryan sacred teachings or exoteric Aryan religion, which was able to encompass and comprehend the All, and therefore also the individual in its arising, working, and passing away to new arising. Such esoteric knowledge was communicated to the folk in symbolically formulated myths, for the naïve popular eye, unaccustomed to such deep vision and clairvoyance, could no more see the primal law than the physical eye can see the whole ocean, or the unschooled inner, spiritual eye the endlessness of life in the All. Therefore the fourteenth rune says: First learn to steer, than dare the sea journey!

Time of the year: October 16 through November 7.

Number: 14

MAN (m)

Exoteric meaning: Man, increase, masculinity, health, plenty, magic.

Esoteric meaning: Spirit, truth, God-Man, male principle in cosmos. Moon, mother, to increase; empty or dead.

MAN is symbolism of man, of mankind, of humanity, of the resurrected god. It signifies the upper part of the world tree Yggdrasill. Rune of spiritual powers, of directing Manna powers. MAN leads to Divine Magic and unfolding of life. It protects against enemies. MAN increases and strengthens the aura. It opens the mysteries of MIMIR, the mysteries of original memories, or of root-memories. Use for levitation, elevation, reaching in the spheres of the Divine.

In another sense, as in that of the well-known folk tale, the man in the moon reveals himself in the fifteenth rune as a sanctified sign of the propagation of the human race. The primal word ma is the hallmark of feminine generation -- mothering -- just as the primal word fa is that of the masculine. Therefore, we have here Mater, mother, just as there we have Fater, father. The moon mythically mystically serves as the magical ring Draupnir, Dripper, from which every ninth night an equally heavy ring drips (separates itself), and which was burned with Baldr; that is, Nanna, the mother of his children, was burned at the same time as Baldr.

According to mythicomystical rules, however, nights always mean months, and so the nine nights mentioned above indicate the time of pregnancy. While the concepts of man, maiden, mother, husband, wife, marriage, menstruation, and so on, and so forth, are rooted in the primal word ma (just like the concept moon, with which they are all internally connected conceptually), they nevertheless symbolize individual concepts reconnected into an apparent unity according to the principle of the multiune multifidic multiplicity. So too is the conceptual word for this unity rooted in the primal word ma and expressed manask or menisk, that is: man (der Mensch).

Therefore--as a concept of unification--the word der Mensch, man, is only of one gender (masculine), while the derogatory concept belongs to the third stage as a neuter, das Mensch, slut, to which we will return later. The fifteenth rune encompasses both the exoteric and esoteric concept of the high mystery of humanity and reaches its zenith in the warning: Be a man!

Time of the year: November 8 through November 29

Number: 15

YR (y, j, ü, ö)

Exoteric meaning: Woman, femininity, desire, sensual love, passion, and perfection.

Esoteric meaning: Woman, mother, chaos from which creation emerges, female principle in the cosmos, God-Woman. Iris, bow, rainbow, yew wood bow, error, anger.

Rune of the unio mystica. Desire for completion, and perfection. Rune of the night and of the Moon. Rune of karma and of karmic tests. The counterpart of MAN, the god with antlers. Roots of the world tree, from which life springs ("the mighty tree which conceals man, where man grew from the roots . . .") God in the waters at the winter solstice. God descending to the material world. YR overcomes illusion of the material world, which is often a painful process bringing radical changes, and a sudden overturning of affairs. Overcomes the illusions of neuro-semantic environments. It recognizes mappings as mappings.

The yr rune is the inverted man rune, and as it designates the bow, so too does it present the waxing and waning moon in contrast to the full moon of the man rune, and so in the first instance it refers to the mutability of the moon, in the second instance as the error rune--referring to the lunar like mutability of the feminine essence, portrayed in later verses of the Lay of the High One in the following way:

The yr rune or error rune, which causes confusion, whether through the excitement of the passions in love, in play, in drink (intoxication), or through pretexts of speech (sophistry) or by whatever other means will perhaps conquer resistance through confusion. But the success of a victory gained by such means is just as illusory as the victory itself--for it brings anger, wild rage, and ultimately madness. The yr rune or error rune therefore also contrasts with the Os rune, since it tries to force the conquest of an opponent with mere pretext instead of with real reasons. Therefore it teaches: Think about the end!

Time of the year: November 30 through December 21.

Number: 16

EH (e)

Exoteric meaning: Marriage, wedding, partnership, permanent bond, binding decision, hope, law, court, duration, horse.

Esoteric meaning: Permanence and marriage as a law, unity of ego and you, sister souls, soul-love, God-Man-Woman.

Rune of cosmic union, which transcends the 16 Runes of the zodiac, or the octagon with its polarities. It is the Rune of ideal love, of twin souls, of soul mates. Two in one, Soul and cosmic. God and man. Connects two lives, brings from the Two to the One. Helps find the soul mate. Brings together soul twins. Brings success and increase.

The seventeenth, or EH rune, plays off against the sixteenth. While that one warns against frivolous transitory love affairs, the marriage rune confirms the concept of lasting love on the basis of marriage as the legal bond between man and woman. This is symbolically indicated by a later EH rune in that the LAF rune is doubled in it, therefore symbolically saying: two bound together by the primal law of life! Marriage is the basis of the folk, and therefore EH is again the concept of law, for, according to an ancient legal formula, marriage is the raw root, that is, the raw root of the continuance of Teutondom. Therefore: Marriage is the raw root of the Aryans!

No connection with the year, referring to polarities unified.

Number: 17

GIBOR (g)

Exoteric meaning: Fulfillment, giver. Gift, sacred marriage, being ONE with the sister soul, protection against evil forces.

Esoteric meaning: God-All, death-life cycle, seeing of the Divine, Being the Divine. The Nordic God, earth; death.

Rune of the wheel of life, of union of the god and the world, of Creator and Created. GIBOR harmonizes the relations of twin souls, unifies the energies of the YOU and I in a cosmic context, both reaching into the common universe, in a true cosmic wedding. Leads to cosmic consciousness, vision of God, unio mystica, the deepest mysteries of the universe.

Gibor altar is still contained in the place name Gibraltar, a name for which the derivation from Arabic gibil tarik is as impossible as it can be; Gib(o)raltar was a temple site consecrated to the Nordic God, the All Begetter by the Vandals at the southern extreme of Spain)--the Nordic God, the All Begetter! -- the Nordic God is the giver, and the earth receives his gifts. But the earth is not only the receiver; she is also in turn a giver. The primal word is gi, or ge; in it lies the idea of arising (to give), but it also indicates being, in the idea of the gift, and passing away to new arising, in the idea of going. This primal word gi or ge can now be connected to other primal and root words, a few examples of which follow. In connection with the primal word fa as: gifa, gefa, gea, geo, it indicates the gift begetting earth, and with bar or bor, burn, spring, the gift burn the Nordic God. As gigeur (the gift goes back to the Primeval), in Gigur, the gift destroying frost giant, who becomes a personification of death and later of the devil, appears to be named. By the idea word gigas (gigeas: the gift goes out of the mouth, out of the source) the fiddle (Geige) is understood. This is the old skaldic magical instrument of awakening which introduced the song, and since song (bar) also means life, the fiddle was one of the many ideographs (hieroglyphs, symbols) of rebirth, and it is for this reason that it is often found in graves as a sacred gift. Therefore it is not necessarily so that the dead man in whose grave a fiddle is found was a fiddle player. Flutes and fiddles enticed people to dance, to the excitement of love, and were therefore banned by the church -- with its ascetic temperament -- because they served as magical instruments to arouse the human fyr, fire, of love. So the church replaced the Wotanic symbol of awakening with the Christian symbol of awakening, the trumpet of judgment. The personal names Gereon and Gertrut are rooted in the primal word ge, meaning rebirth, and the hieroglyph of this, the Head of Gereon, appears as an equilateral triangle made of three human profiles.

But this Gereon is, in turn, the Nordic God incarnate in the All as the All Spirit, World Spirit or Human Spirit. And for this reason the meaning of the ge rune is closest to that of the fyrfos. The difference between the two interpretations lies in the fact that the idea of the ge rune or Gibor rune seeks exoterically to approach the comprehension of the idea of the divine from below upward--in a certain sense from the level of humanity outward--while the explanation of the fyrfos seeks knowledge of the Nordic God esoterically in the innermost level of man himself -- and finds it. Thus it is known, as the spirit of humanity, to be unified with the Nordic God from the standpoint of the concept of the bifidic biune dyad, and it will attain certain knowledge from inside out, as well as toward the inside from the outside. Here again the exoteric and the esoteric are clearly distinguished, and the fyrfos is recognized as an exoteric secret sign of high holiness, which is represented exoterically by the Ge rune. So, while the exoteric doctrine teaches that man emerged from the Nordic God and will return to the Nordic God, the esoteric doctrine knows the invisible cohesion of man and divinity as the bifidic biune dyad--and so it can be consciously said: "Man--be one with the Nordic God!"

GIBOR has no relation to any part of the zodiac, but it is Symbolism of wholeness.

Number: 18

The Runic Sky
Allan Webber

One of the mysteries surrounding the Norse Vikings is the lack of evidence of a knowledge of astronomy. As a seafaring race with an economy dependent on fickle weather patterns it would seem inconceivable that there was no interest in the stars. In the Prose Edda by Snorri Sturluson (c1120 AD) he records as part of ancestral belief.

"Similarly they learned from their elderly relatives that after many hundreds of years had been reckoned there was the same earth, sun and heavenly bodies. But the courses of the heavenly bodies were various, some had a longer course and some a shorter. From such things they thought it likely that there must be some controller of the heavenly bodies who must be regulating their courses in accordance with his will." - Prologue

The absence of evidence suggests that, given its importance, it was a hidden knowledge so highly revered it could not be made public. In an oral society such as existed up to the end of the first millennium it placed a large burden on the mechanisms available to transmit knowledge. The meaning of words and plays on sound were crucial. The runes were one piece of evidence left by early Vikings and it would not therefore be surprising to find they have highly structured, astronomic meaning.

This paper presents some of the results of my research into the hidden astronomy. It presents a table of the well established runes with the name(s) for the star group(s) of each. These are then shown on star maps to show how they fill the sky, are mapped easily using all the brightest stars and how they need minimal distortion, inversion or rotation to place each rune. I then give some other reasons for my selection based on the fit between the meaning of the rune, the attributes of the star groups, the stories linked to the star groups and the names of the stars.

Runes of the elder Futhark and their place in the sky.

There are 24 runes in the elder futhark and the shapes are those used in the early to middle part of the first millenium. The names are not necessarily from that period for at this time the Scandinavian society relied on oral transmission of knowledge.

Fehu Pegasus	Uruz Aries	Thurisaz Cepheus	Ansuz Cassiopia	Raido Draco	Kenaz Cancer	Gebo Bootes & Virgo	Wunjo Cygnus & Lyra
Hagelaz Taurus	Naudhiz Eridanus	Isa Polestar	Jera Gemini	Eiwaz PolarWheel	Perthro Perseus	Elhaz Auriga	Sowilu U.Major East
Tiwaz U.major Central	Berkano U.Major West	Ehwaz Hercules	Mannaz Orion	Laguz Cetus	Ingwaz Triangulum	Othala Andromeda	Dagaz Moon

The star names given in the table were not chosen solely by looking for patterns that fit. The process involved:

A belief the Runes may have been astronomic based

Grouping Runes based on their meaning – Sun references implied stars linked to summer

Choosing star patterns where clear wording exist

A belief the names of the Runes may have been influenced by the Viking's contact with people knowledgeable in Arabic astronomy

Filling in the gaps with the most appropriate patterns

Examples of the use of runic meaning in choosing star pattern:

The most distinctive meanings can be seen in **Raido, Tiwaz** and **Eiwaz** for these have direct astronomical linking.

Raido is traditionally associated with circular or spiral journeys and is linked to the wheeling of stars around the cosmic axis. Draco serves this role throughout history and even as the wheel of precession turns, its shape twists around the pole.

Tiwaz has association with the spear or pointer and the god Týr. It is seen as a guiding principle, steadfast and able to be used in judging one's position. In the Old English Rune Poem Týr is a star. Throughout the first two millennia Dubhe and Merek in Ursa Major have been called 'The Pointers' for they indicate the position of the Polestar and were used by mariners and travelers to find their position.

Eiwaz represents the spinning World Tree, Yggdrasill. It is the axis about which all else revolves. Eiwaz is based on either the annual axis (celestial pole) or the 25,000 year processional axis (terrestrial pole). In my presentation it has a meaning different from most of the other rune figures for it (and Isa) represent an astronomic principal more than a single location. However, its shape can be seen dominating the axes of the sky.

The material presented offers a strong visual proof of its merits. Any other evidence is purely supportive. I therefore proceed directly to the Futhark and the signs in the sky.

The Runic sky in 1200AD October 20th, midnight had the following appearance:

LOOKING TOWARD THE NORTH

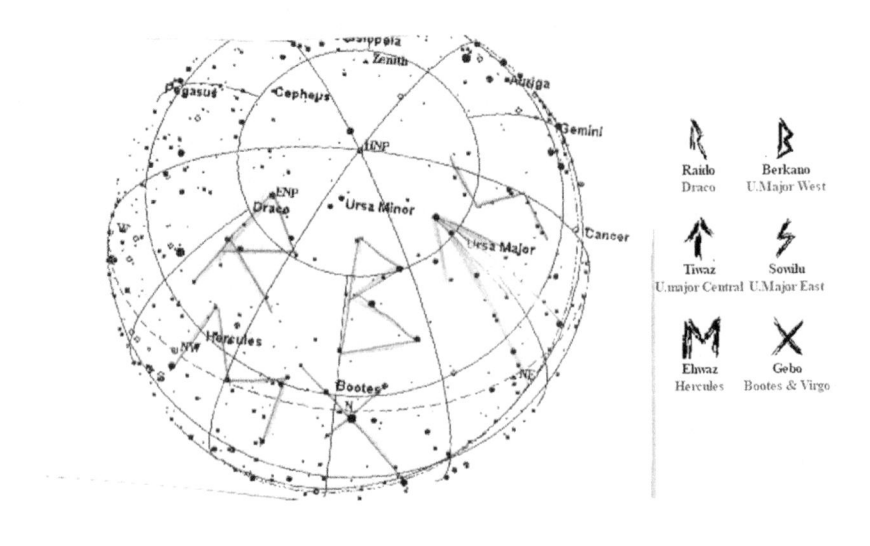

LOOKING TOWARD THE EAST SOUTHEAST

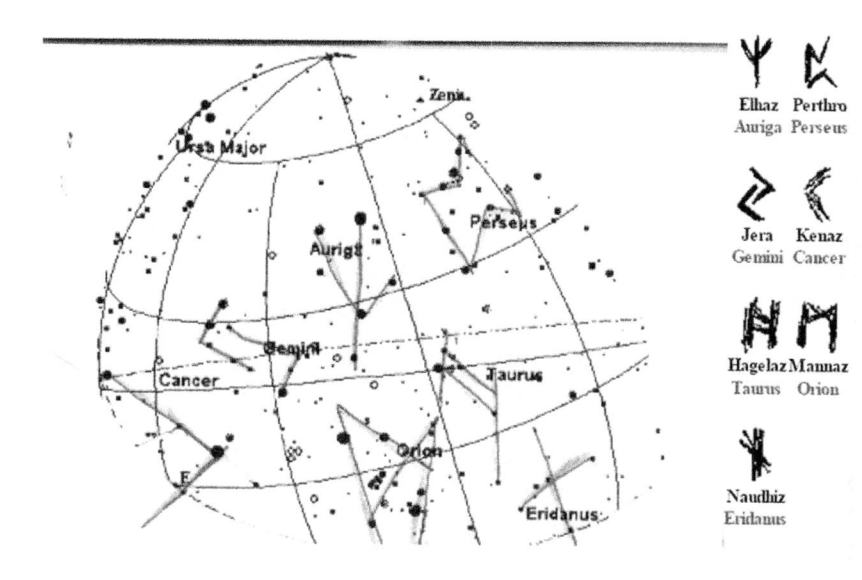

Elhaz — Auriga
Perthro — Perseus
Jera — Gemini
Kenaz — Cancer
Hagelaz — Taurus
Mannaz — Orion
Naudhiz — Eridanus

LOOKING TOWARD THE WEST SOUTHWEST

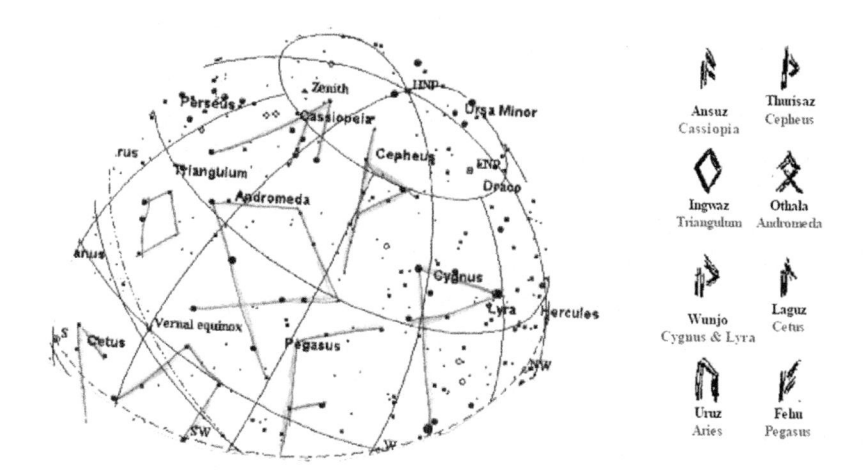

Ansuz — Cassiopia
Thurisaz — Cepheus
Ingwaz — Triangulum
Othala — Andromeda
Wunjo — Cygnus & Lyra
Laguz — Cetus
Uruz — Aries
Fehu — Pegasus

LOOKING TO THE ZENITH

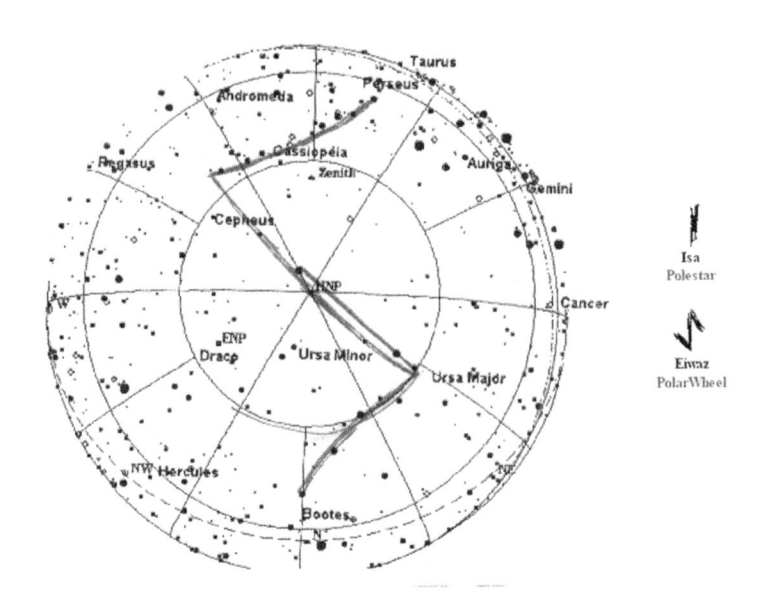

The hypothesis underlying this work is that the runes were based on images in the sky. These rune pictures are likely to be from times well before the end of the first millennium but the names are a later addition. By the beginning of the second millennium the Vikings had substantive contact with Western civilization (for example The Prose Edda by Snorri Sturluson contains quite lengthy stories of Troy). They had quite lengthy contact with other European nations from their Viking settlements in England, Scotland, Ireland and France. The Norse had a long history in navigation and hence is likely to have been keenly interested in astronomy. The ideas of the Arabic world were the source for astronomy at this time. To serve their own ends and advance their astronomy it is possible that they infused the meaning and names to link the two systems (Norse & Arabic/ancient) together. All of this is hinted at in the continuation of the quotation from the prologue of Snorri Sturluson's Prose Edda:

"And so they believed that he ruled all things on earth and in the sky, of heaven and the heavenly bodies, of the sea and the weathers. But so as to be better able to give an account of this and fix it in memory, they then gave a name among themselves to everything, and this religion has changed in many ways as nations became distinct and languages branched."

Despite the suggestion of a 'memory science' based on names there is no established body of evidence for Viking astronomy. The above hypothesis is an acceptance of the logic of an astronomic science concealed within the tools of the oral and runic tradition. In the following I list ways in which this hypothesis guided my selections.

The rationale underlying my original choice of runes:

The first rune chosen (after the clearly astronomic runes) was **Hagelaz**. Hagelaz represents hail and this is in turn referred to as an egg, the cosmic egg. But the cosmic egg is also a classical allusion referring to Taurus for the bull held the egg within its horns. An examination of the rising of Taurus shows that October is the month when it rose as the sun set. October 20th leads on to winter's depths making the hail emblem very appropriate. This choice underlay the selection of October 20th for my astronomic charts. Hagelaz may have linguistic links to the Arabic name for the lead star in Taurus 'Hadl al hajm' known more commonly as Aldebaran.

As Taurus rises Lyra is at the meridian and Bootes is setting. At midnight on October 20th Taurus moves to the meridian and Cancer is rising. It is likely that if Taurus is a seasonal reference identified by 'hail' then the runes for Cancer, Lyra and Bootes will contain appropriate symbols.

Gebo is seen as a form of the solar wheel. It celebrates the changing of the seasons and the gifts of grain and wealth from the gods. It emphasizes partnership between giver and receiver, a mutual union. This hints of spring, fertilization and the utilization of personal effort in the sowing and nurturing of seed. Gebo should then be seen as a union of Bootes and Virgo for it is these that rise over the horizon in spring. The pattern for Gebo is X. To build this image requires both Bootes and Virgo. It is possibly not just a physical union for the name may result from combining elements of Virgo ('g') and Bootes ('bo').

Wunjo is connected with 'wind' and similarly to winter. It represents happiness, joy, glory, victory and companionship but more importantly changes in direction. These activities, especially companionship are dominant in winter and joy and victory may reflect on activities of this enclosed season. The linguistic link of Wunjo to winter is quite strong but there may also be links to the Arabic name for Lyra, 'Al Sanja'. The name and the winter appearance of Lyra and Cygnus form the basis of the association with Wunjo. Ophiuccus is also a candidate for it is in the winter sector below Lyra. The rune may stretch across more than one constellation and may be larger and much lower than shown in my runic sky picture

Kenar *(= Kenaz: z and r are represented by same letter)* represents a torch that transforms and regenerates. It is a primal force within the creation myth whereby fire and ice are generators of the life force. And Cancer is the constellation that is linked to the furthest northward movement of the sun. Before the appearance of Cancer on the horizon the sun moves north. After its appearance the sun is transformed and moves back along its previous path (like a crab). Therefore the torch can be seen as the sun in summer when its burning powers are strong and the transformation and regeneration is its turning and retracing of its earlier path. In addition there seems to be a possible linguistic link between Kenar and Cancer. Also the nearby Canis Minor and Major seem involved. The torch could be Sirius the brightest star in the sky.

There are other methods of determining a connection. One of these is the significance of the sign rather than its pattern. The rune for Jera is a good example.

Jera is a twinned pair ⟨⟩. It is the only rune of this nature. As such it represents Gemini. Its meaning is the fruitful completion of a cycle, a season or year. It is the harvest symbol and is faithfully represented by Gemini, which lies between the summer rune of Cancer and the mid autumn rune of Taurus. Its name Jera or its alternate form 'Jeza' has connection to the Arabic name (Al Jeuze).

The link between the runic name and the Arabic name is also a source of connection as it has been in each of the foregoing examples. It is not enough on its own, but it is often an indicative element.

Bercano seems clearly linked to 'Banat Nash al Kubra', a name for Ursa Major. Bercano is the rune associated with birth and rebirth. It is the Great Mother, the Earth Goddess and linked to the renewal of spring. This places it immediately above the spring constellations of Bootes and Virgo (Gebo) and again this is the western end of the Great Bear or Ursa Major.

Raido was one of the first runes mentioned in this paper. It is a clear astronomic rune linked to Draco. The Arabic names 'Draconis', 'Al Rakis', 'Alwaid' used in this constellation form an additional linguistic link.

Naudhiz has the runic significance of controlling the fates. The Norns were based at the foot of the trunk of Yggdrasill and watered its roots from the fountain of 'Urd'. Eridanus has linguistic connection to Naudhiz and Urd. Eridanus is also known as 'Al Nahr' and 'Nahar'. Eridanus fits well to the description of the 'fountain of Urd'. Eridanus is known as ' the river' and only the northern edge of the river shows in the high North skies. It is a band that hugs the horizon and could be rightly described as being a fountain at the foot of the astronomical tree. The stars that never rise contain the bulk of Eridanus and it therefore provides the water for the sustenance of the roots forever buried beneath the earth.

Laguz is Al Kaitos. The runic Laguz represents the sea and other bodies of water and one of the others wells of the Norns, 'the well of Wyrd'. Cetus is a sea monster, a weird marine animal that again is only visible on the Nordic horizon. The associative link between Ursa Major and Bootes (Bercano and Gebo) discussed earlier provides another strong group of linkages. Bercano and Gebo are linked by the season of spring. This seasonal reference can be extended to Cancer and Sowilo as summer runes.

Sowilo is the rune linked to the sun. This is clearly a summer rune and places it above Kenar or Cancer. This is the eastern part of Ursa Major. Sometimes the link is somewhat deeper as in the case of 'the cosmic egg' for Hagelaz. Uruz, Isa and Eiwaz also have such interpretation.

Uruz is associated with the primal creative force and refers to the 'earliest' or 'original' element, sound or item. Uruz has linguistic links to Aries and this constellation contains 'the first point of Aries' a traditional astronomic label for the first star that used to rise over the horizon at the vernal equinox. Aries is the 'original' or 'earliest' starting point for astronomy and therefore fits to the meaning of Uruz.

Isa is the primal ice, glacial in nature seeming static but imperceptibly mobile. The ice identifies the north and in particular the North Pole and the rune's ice properties fit to that of the Polestar. The precession of the heavens takes 25,000 years and during that time stars such as Thuban, Cyanosura and Vega become the Polestar. The change from one to another takes thousands of years and each appears fixed at the pole from year to year. At present Cyanosura, known also as Polaris and Navigatori is as close as it will ever be to the Celestial North Pole. The Isa rune describes a single star and its rune figure, a single line, may well be from the Polestar to the pole.

Eiwaz is the spinning World Tree, the axis around which all revolves. Earlier this was identified as an overriding pattern describing the larger pattern of movement around the pole. This is reinforced by another image for the rune Eiwaz. In Valkyrie (see credits) it says, "It suggests the passage and communication between different worlds and layers of reality"

Other runes rely on the combination of linguistic links, astronomic meaning, seasonal placement and suggestive imagery.

Thurisaz (Phurisaz) is seen as a rune for defense and destruction with links to thorns and castles, shields and the rescue of captives, victims and the besieged. Cepheus, the king of Ethiopia, after whom the constellation Cepheus is named, was the father of Andromeda. Andromeda was rescued by Perseus after she was chained to a rock by the Nereids, who were enraged by claims by Andromeda's mother that she was more beautiful than they. The Arabic names for Cepheus include 'Phirceus' ,'Phicareus' and 'Ficares'

Perthro is the rune of the warrior who constantly tests himself against chance and luck. Perseus was a warrior who not only pitted himself against the forces of nature to rescue Andromeda but who had previously beheaded the Medusa, whose face could turn those who looked on it to stone. It was Medusa's head with its snake like hair that Perseus used in the rescue of Andromeda. Surely Perseus is a warrior who constantly tested himself against chance and luck. Perseus and Perthro have similar sounds suggesting a possible common origin.

Ophala is the rune of the village, homeland and family. It is the family group and its inheritance, customs, duties and language. It is the inherited wealth that comes from one's ancestors. Andromeda had no other claim to fame other than the looks and title that she inherited and it was her homeland as well as Andromeda herself that suffered by her mother's boasting of their inherited attributes. The lead star of Andromeda is 'Alpheratz'.

Ehwaz is the rune associated with twin gods, heroes or horses. Sleipnir is the name of the horse and represents fertility and partnership. Sleipnir was an eight-legged grey horse that could cross land and sea. It typified the wind, which blows from the eight cardinal points of the compass. In the legend of Perseus, the winged horse Pegasus is born out of the blood of Medusa spilled at the time she was beheaded. Pegasus was born at the time of Perseus' battle against Neptune who also created a horse, Arion. This horse possessed human feet for its right legs, it spoke with a human voice and ran with incredible swiftness. Arion became the horse of the hero Hercules. Here then are the twin horses and twin heroes; Perseus and Hercules, Arion and Pegasus. The combined properties of these horses are then found in Sleipnir.

Fehu is the rune of fruitfulness and wealth associated with animal husbandry. The god Freyr is closely linked to the rune and this God had a horse called Bloodhoof. Pegasus was born out of the blood of Medusa. The constellation of Pegasus contains names Alfares, Faras al Thani, Enifr, Alanf, Fum Alfares that seem to relate to Fehu and Freyr.

The remaining star pattern/runes have the following seeds underlying their union.

Mannaz is the rune of mortality representing individuals or groups. To link this rune of mortality to an ancient star pattern is not difficult. A long tradition makes Orion, the Hunter, a logical choice. It is Orion that was the focus of the Egyptian union of mortal man with immortal stars. The major star of Orion is called Misan (al Batil).

Elhaz implies a two edged sword and is a sign to promote victory and protection. This is a warrior rune and naturally draws the attention to Auriga, the charioteer where the sword is a major weapon of a warrior thought to bring both victory and protection. Auriga contains 'Alcahela' and is known as 'Alhajor' or 'Elhajor'.

Ingwaz is associated with marking out the boundaries. Its relevant gods circuit the bounds of the land ensuring their fertility. Triangulum marks the boundaries of autumn and winter and the boundary of the bountiful bright stars in the Milky Way and the less spectacular other regions of the heavens. Its name 'Triangulum' contains the critical 'ng/gn' sound associated with this rune.

Ansuz is the rune of inspired speech, the passing of knowledge in an orally based society. It is the rune of the poet and the seer. These references suggest that Ansuz is Hermes, the messenger of speech, and therefore represents the planet Mercury that is also known by the name Hermes. It is quite likely some or all runes have planetary significance as well as representing fixed stars. Cassiopeia's claim to fame was from her words through boasting of her own and Andromeda's inherited beauty. Such speech seems hardly inspiring or poetic but more provocative. Despite this I chose Ansuz for Cassiopeia because after all my other selections Ansuz remained unplaced and yet it fitted elegantly to the gap in the sky left by the other runic figures.

http://alynptyltd.tripod.com/TheRunicSky/TheRunicSky.htm

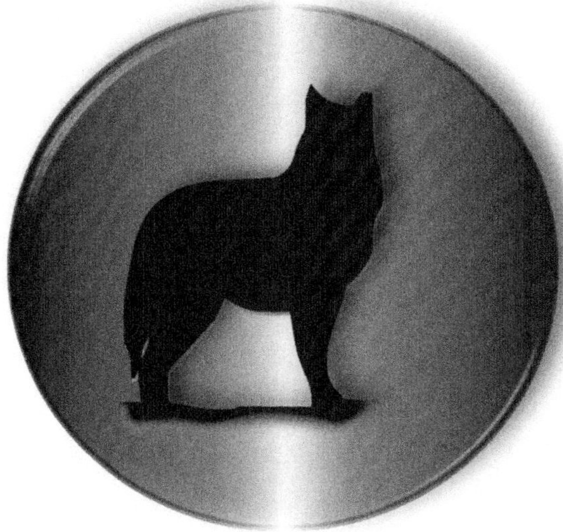

Allen Hartley

About the Author

Allen Hartley has always been fascinated with ancient cultures and societies. He has spent decades researching the subject matter and continues to gravitate back to his favorites; the early societies of the Northern Celts, Nordics, and the Egyptians. For over ten years, Allen has focused on the Runic scripts of these societies. In particular, their formations, vibrations, meanings, and usage.

Allen has dual degrees in technology and engineering, spending more than eighteen years in research and development, system and network design, programming, integration and deployment, disaster recovery, and production support. Changing mindsets and styles from technical writing to fictional writing has been a tremendous challenge for Allen.

With the technology bust, he left the field in 2002 to settle in North Idaho with his wife and son.

For more than a decade, Allen has continued to pursue his research and ideas as a series of books began to evolve. While his current employment requires extensive travel, it allowed him to publish his first book, Secrets of the Soul in 2012. The second book, Mists of Dawn was published in 2013 and was a challenge due to his unpredictable schedule. The third book in the series, Boundaries of Time was released in 2014 and required an enormous amount of time researching the background material. Once again, his unpredictable schedule also posed a challenge in completing the book. Also released in 2014 was a joint project with his wife, Vanessa, Nature's Palette – Waterscapes. This is a coffee table picture book inspired by their Celtic ancestry.

The concepts for the current book, Journey of a Celtic Soul emerged from the research for the first three works of fictional history. Journey of a Celtic Soul is the author's reflections of his multiple iterations through this dimensional universe. The whisperings of his ancestors and the dimensional universe coupled with his recovered memories from past lives have contributed to the material for the book.

Each time, his wife, Vanessa, has been a great source to help refine his ideas on the graphics, story, extra material, and of course as a reviewer of the book.

Printed in Great Britain
by Amazon